Living in the
Key West Style
anywhere!

D1310743

David L. Hemmel, PE
and
Judi Sample Smith, AIBD

Duval Publishing
Key West, Florida

Publisher's Cataloging-in-Publication
(Provided by Quality Books, Inc.)

Hemmel, David L.
    Living in the Key West style anywhere! / David L.
Hemmel and Judi Sample Smith.
    p. cm.
    Includes bibliographical references.
    ISBN 0-9745637-0-6

    1. Architecture, Domestic--Florida--Key West.
2. Architecture, Tropical--Florida--Key West.
3. Vernacular architecture--Florida--Key West. 4. Key West
(Fla.)--Buildings, structures, etc. I. Smith, Judi
Sample. II. Title.

NA7238.K48H46 2004   728'.37'0975941
                QBI03-200767
Printed in Hong Kong

Duval Publishing
P.O. Box 4255
Key West, Florida 33041
Tel: 1/800-355-8562
Web: www.southerncoastaldesigns.com

Acknowledgments

Without the tireless and determined efforts of so many Key West citizens over the past decades, the beautiful old homes of our city might have disappeared, as they have in other communities. For the opportunity to become intimately acquainted and write about these residential monuments, we are grateful to organizations such the Old Island Restoration Foundation, the Historic Architectural Review Commission, and the many individual citizens who continue to protect this southernmost heritage.

One of the most enjoyable aspects of researching material for this book was the opportunity to meet many of Key West's talented homeowners and craftsmen who share a passion for restoring and preserving these faded treasures. In particular, I would like to acknowledge the various contributions of Don Gray, Gregor Tausche, Bob Kruse, Jay Fairbanks, Dawn Thornburgh, Joyce Stahl, George Halloran and Armando Ramirez,. In addition, the Heritage House, Curry Mansion, Alexander's Guest House, Pejuta, and the staffs of the Monroe County Extension Service and Key West Garden Club were very helpful. Tom Hambright, Director of Local and State History of the Monroe County Library at Key West, patiently allowed yet another would-be author to spend months searching through his extensive files and materials. John Preston and Bill Renner were kind enough to point us in all the right directions in our research of the New Urbanism movement and offer their opinions on this subject.

One of the truly essential contributors to this project was Len Buckwalter who, with his wife Mary, has been a longtime friend and advisor. His assistance in the editing, layout and publishing tasks was, as always, very professional, and his advice we learned years ago to accept without question.

And finally, thank you Susie Rafferty and Ron Smith for your patience and encouragement.

Contents

Chapter 1

"How I Found Me a Home"

"Have we passed that house before? I wonder who lives in these ramshackle old mansions with their long porches and treetop widow's walks?" That was my first impression while wandering around the old, disorienting neighborhoods of Key West. We hoped to eventually stumble onto Duval Street, our real destination, and all my mental resources were bent to the task. Like most first-time visitors we had not been drawn to Key West by the architecture.

Years later I arrived for what would become a permanent stay, and I began to see this seaport town in a new light. The crew on my sailboat, Carioca, were sent home. In the words of a local songwriter "I had found me a home." Something indefinable about the gracious old neighborhoods and people worked its magic on yet another visitor and, in a couple of more years, I was once again a landlubber. The modest cottage I chose would need a lot of love and all my renovation skills, but in the end I'd be rewarded by a feeling of easy comfort lacking in all the modern structures I'd owned before.

Stripping away the patina of decades of neglect turned into a fascinating discovery process. Pulling interior siding boards from walls I would expose long-forgotten building techniques. Peering under the crawl space revealed cypress stumps logged nearly a century ago yet still solid. I was hooked, and my interest stirred in all the old houses around Key West. Books I found on the subject gave some order and cataloging to the various house styles, and more than one had stunning frontal photographs. But I wanted to lift the captains' walks and tin roofs off the mansions and humble shotguns to view the interior architecture of structures where Key West's famous and forgotten had called home.

This book attempts to build on many fine works already published and fill additional needs I felt were left unanswered. Whether you're a prospective resident or simply a curious visitor, I hope the following pages will add to your understanding and love of the old Key West Conch houses. Maybe you'll find new ideas and stimulation for that renovation job you've been contemplating. Perhaps you've found something special on this island that you would love to recreate in another location. In this case, detailed house plans for both classic Conch houses and more contemporary versions are readily available in the listings at the end. No matter what your housing plans, I hope you eventually enjoy living in the Key West Style as much as we do!

Chapter 2

So You'd Like to Own a Conch House

What would it be like to live along Southard Street, walking down to Five Brothers for Cuban coffee each morning?

Each year some 1.5 million tourists discover Key West. They come to enjoy the nearly perfect year round weather, beaches, water sports, or special events such as Fantasy Fest and Hemingway Days. Asking directions from the first local they encounter, some make a beeline for one of the most popular streets in America, Duval, with her round-the-clock party. Others may have selected Key West to temporarily retreat from 21st century bustle in a quiet tropical setting. Eventually, both groups discover the gentle charm of Key West's neighborhoods with their historic frame houses. Mo-

torized trollies, trains, bicycle and walking tours introduce the visitor to grand Victorian mansions, more modest two stories with inviting verandas, and tiny cottages appealingly embellished with gingerbread trim. Their past ownership by artists, writers, actors and other notables who lived side by side with working class Conchs are enumerated. The visitor inevitably leaves with warm memories of these charming homes, their picket fences enclosing the green lushness of palm, and exploding colors of Bougainvillea and Royal Poinciana.

Co-author Dave Hemmel in front of his Southard Street cottage.

The Queen Conch

Those mainlanders may have their bald eagle, but in Key West the Conch is king, or should I say queen? They're a very appropriate symbol for Key Westers---hard crusted and able to survive any of life's upsets. They simply stick their toe into the sand, laboriously set their world right side up, and begin inching along again. Today they are emblazoned across our flags, symbolized by our high school athletic teams, adorn our restaurants and liquor stores, and even have a style of housing named after them. What is this animal we hear of so often but so seldom see?

Your first experience with a Conch was probably as a child, when your aunt and uncle returning from a Florida vacation held a shell to your ear so you could "hear the ocean". There's an excellent chance that shell was from the *Strombus Gigas* or Queen Conch family. This relative of the snail has been around 65 million years and is found as far south as Brazil and as far north as Bermuda. They're numerous throughout the West Indies and Bahamas and, until recent decades, in the Florida Keys.

A Conch reaches a mature size of 8 to 12 inches and 5 pounds after 4 years. They favor shallow grass beds, pulling themselves along slowly with the aid of a small hornlike "operculum" at the base of their foot while grazing on grasses, algae and floating organic debris. They've joined the endangered species list in the United States and much of the Conch we now enjoy come from the Bahamas or Turks and Caicos, where they are still harvested in the wild and farmed commercially.

Early Bahamian settlers were fond of the delicious meat which could be tenderized (or cracked) and fried with batter. They're also tasty in a chowder or eaten raw. Far out islanders sometimes dry the meat in the sun, yielding a tough and unusually spicy jerky. Today they remain a major food source for Bahamians, with half a million pounds consumed annually in addition to the large amount exported to the United States. Many a sailor has grown to prefer Conch over other seafood choices in large part because they are easily

The Queen Conch *(Stombus gigas).*

scooped up wherever he drops anchor. A delicious salad is made by combining raw, sliced Conch with sour orange, lime, peppers, onion, tomato and salt. Some prize the Conch's long transparent tube called the "pistol" or "style" for its reputed Viagra-like characteristics.

The Conch shell is also a valuable commodity used for decoration or fashioned into jewelry. Like an oyster, the Conch can produce a "pearl" that is beautiful, rare, and will fetch as much as $1000 on the market. These pearls cannot be cultured and are usually discovered by biting into your cracked Conch dinner. Saw the tip off a Conch shell and - *voila!* - you have a musical instrument. Each year Key West holds a contest to establish the champion virtuoso on this Conch "horn".

So the favorite of our founding fathers has considerable to distinguish it. Not as noble as the lion or swift as the deer, it is nevertheless our own true Key West royalty - the Queen Conch.

A feeling of envy for the gracious eccentrics observed on front porch swings or bicycling down quiet lanes follows the visitors back to their northern-based apartments, condominiums, and tract house neighborhoods. "What would it be like to live along Southard Street, walking down to Five Brothers for Cuban coffee each morning, riding a bicycle to the post office and being greeted by smiling neighbors from their porches and windows."

These fantasies lead many to plan longer vacations to this tropical port each year. Finally, some career alteration or early retirement opportunity leads them to consider the unthinkable: actually making a lifestyle change and purchasing one of the Conch houses of Key West. That first weekend with the real estate agent leaves the prospective owners stunned by the price tags of Key West real estate. It seems thousands of others had the same fantasies and got here first. But, bolstered with the knowledge that few people have ever lost money on Key West real estate and a large number have become quite wealthy, they make the commitment and become the new owners of a small, slightly threadbare house with great renovation possibilities.

Since the once cult recording "Wasting Away in Margaritaville" brought a new generation of curious visitors to this southernmost island, the above scenario has been played out over and over. The elegant wooden frame neighborhoods so reminiscent of America's small town roots but also representing something slightly exotic and mysterious from our past have drawn thousands of new transplants since 1980. They come from

every walk of life in America and also from European and Latin cultures.

But while the fascinating houses and neighborhoods of Key West may have changed these transplants, the reverse is equally true. In his 1968 article "The Carpenter Architects of Key West" Roger Starr wrote that Key West was at a critical crossroads and mused whether the next decade would see the demise of the old dilapidated historical buildings or whether they would be protected, restored, and preserved. He would be happy with the path history has taken. Today it is hard to find a Conch house without a new coat of paint, restored facades, and well-manicured patio. An untouched relic is constantly sought by a small army of renovation-minded residents.

But these renovations must be executed with consideration for tradition and historical appearances. Without dictating excessive uniformity, a Historic Architecture Review Committee has assured that the important historic features of houses are retained and the character of Old Town preserved. Inside their Conch house, however, the owners have had fewer restrictions to limit their imagination, and some truly beautiful and innovative restorations can be viewed on the periodic house tours sponsored by the Old Island Restoration Foundation.

So with proper permits in hand, the new owners of a Conch house will begin the dusty work of renovation but soon discover it to be a delightful experience. As one explores the crawlspace beneath the first floor, a child's doll, a rare bottle from the 1930s or other astonishing treasure will be unearthed. Peeling up 1950s

A neighborhood meeting place. This one-room grocery is a pleasant reminder of the days before supermarkets. It's also a favorite for morning *con lechi*, *bucci* and conversation.

Before

The elderly resident of this rambling home, famous for its gingerbread man trim, never failed to give me a friendly smile and an interesting story about old Key West. Today, new owners have taken on the responsibiity of preserving and renewing this unique piece of vernacular architecture.

After

linoleum, an intact tongue and groove floor of oak or Dade county pine may be revealed that only awaits sandpaper, stain and varnish to recover its long forgotten beauty. Walls of horizontally laid 1 x 4 boards, whether painted or stripped to display the warmth of reddish Dade County pine, give a unique feel forgotten since the introduction of plasterboard and processed wood panels decades ago. The astonishing amount of renovation activity at least partially explains how 25,478 residents supposedly under a building moratorium have been able to support two lumber yards, four hardware stores, 16 architects and 47 general contractors.

Of the 2580 residences in the Historic District of Key West almost all have undergone some degree of transformation. While nostalgia for the old days is inevitable, the revived neighborhoods and other cul-

tural improvements have led more than one life-long resident to confide that they enjoy Key West today more than at any other time in their lives.

But not all the appealing wood frame homes one finds in Key West represent old construction. When a large section of Old Town known as the Truman annex was transferred from the Navy to the public sector, the residential construction that followed was accomplished so as to tastefully blend with the historic residences. Key features of the Conch houses were duplicated and the flavor of the older neighborhoods retained. This was all accomplished, of course, using modern materials and construction methods. So as one walks the streets of Truman Annex today one is greeted with the elegant temple, distinctive eyebrow, and octagonal turrets of the Victorian. Behind picket fences residents

Key West's Truman Annex.

enjoy the congeniality of verandas, front porch swings, second story galleries that open off bedrooms, and the sound of the afternoon showers' patter on tin roofs. The reproduction of these interesting house styles has not been limited to just the island of Key West. Up the Florida Keys, around the Gulf coast, in fact, across the nation similar development projects are blossoming. The community of Seaside, Florida made famous in the movie, The Truman Show, was one of the earliest projects. These developments are influenced by a movement known as New Urbanism that has arisen to address many of the woes of our residential environments. Concepts such as narrow pedestrian-friendly streets, small neighborhoods with town squares and easily accessible services, and houses with front porches close to the sidewalks are being promoted. In short, a return to what Key Westers have always known was the only way to live. It appears Americans view the traditional house styles differently today, and architects are no longer hesitant to design vernacular-type homes.

"But is this wood frame style house a practical, modern choice? I'd like to live in a cozy version of

What is Dade County Pine?

The first thing a realtor points out in an old Conch house is the "Dade County Pine". But what exactly is it? What's so great about it, and where does one obtain it? Local residents to whom I posed these questions often gave me a puzzled look. So I did some research. Dade County Pine (*pinus elliottii var. densa*) really is a separate species, or more properly subspecies, of the Longleaf Yellow Pine (*pinus*

palustris), which is more commonly known as Heart Pine. In the 1800's vast forests stretched from southeast Virginia to Florida and around the gulf coast to eastern Texas. It was said that a squirrel could travel down the east coast to Florida without ever touching the ground. It was North America's version of the Amazon rain forest, and the supply seemed endless. By the 1920's, these forests were essentially gone with only about 2% remaining today.

What made this slow-growing variety so desirable as a construction material was its very high heart wood content. The tree is nearly all heart wood core as opposed to the outer sapwood. It is this high content of the resinous heart wood that makes the species so rigid and strong and accounts for its inherent resistance to rot and insects. The country was literally built on Heart Pine at least in the southeastern part of the United States. In fact, the decking and keel on America's most famous ship, Old Ironsides, which still floats today, were constructed from this sturdy tree.

The subspecies, Dade County Pine, grew between the Everglades and the Atlantic ocean and even on some of the northern keys. It has the same interesting appearance and is even more dense. The wood is actually white when cut, and takes on the familiar reddish tone when exposed to air. The virgin forests are largely extinct for both species, and most commercially available material comes from companies specializing in reclaimed wood (see the Resource section of this book).

The tree shown here is part of a second growth stand located in Long Pine Key in the Florida Everglades.

Rain on a Tin Roof

Some believe Key Westers switched to tin roofs because of the disastrous fire of 1886. I know this isn't true. It is because of the wonderful sound that a tin roof makes during our daily summertime downpours. When I notice those first dark cumulus beginning to close ranks, I know it's time for a break from whatever I'm doing, and I head for my side porch. If it's late enough in the afternoon, perhaps I'll mix a cocktail. On the porch, I ease into a padded bamboo chair and gaze upward. There's no ceiling between myself and the 26 Gauge metal panels nailed to a white framework. The first heavy drops begin to crash loudly onto the roof and splash against the street pavement out front raising miniature dust clouds. The air is suddenly chilled from the downdraft within the cumulus nimbus. The cool mass spreading horizontally has made a spectacular descent after reaching heights of maybe 15,000 to 20,000 feet. Now the noise level becomes deafening, blanketing. The indefinable smell of the rain is everywhere, and the sounds of the street, the city, the whole world are drowned out. In fact, except for my immediate yard, the rest of the world isn't even visible. The water pouring

Caroline Street, from a dry seat under the metal roof at B.O.'s Fish Wagon

over the end of the tin roof is a solid sheet. A view of Niagara from the underside. Soon the roar begins to lessen a bit. Nature's orchestra is nearing the end of another crescendo. But the world will be left cleaner, refreshed, renewed. In a short time, Key West's roofs are again sparkling in the afternoon sun like pieces of a shattered mirror sprinkled over a lush, green blanket

Tennessee Williams' cottage but is it as durable and maintainable as other housing alternatives?" In the 300 block of Duval Street sits a modest one and one-half story frame residence constructed around 1829 and later owned by Capt. Francis Watlington. During its 173-year history, it survived 11 hurricanes and the high winds of countless tropical storms. Despite the threat of fire, flood, tropical climate, and an area of significant termite risk, it stands straight and solid. It's constructed entirely of wood, which has always been a traditional American building material from colonial times. Wood continues to offer many advantages: very high strength to weight characteristics and easily worked by beginner or experienced carpenter. When repairs or modifications are required, they are more easily accomplished with wood homes than homes of any other material. Maintenance associated with the wood frame house has also been considerably reduced. Paint is applied with much less effort, frequently requiring only one coat, and it lasts for years.

While today's treated lumber offers many prob-

lem-free years, alternative siding choices are now available that are truly maintenance-free and virtually indistinguishable from real wood. Modern windows and doors are available in vinyl-clad colors that retain a traditional appearance.

So as you turn the following pages, learn a bit more about the old wood frame homes of Key West and their unique architecture. Indulge your fantasies for a moment---whether they're about new construction or breathing life into your plain old house with some Key West style. Which of the more than 100 gingerbread patterns (shown at the end) should grace your front porch? Or imagine your home surrounded by the profusion of colors in the Garden section, with tropical fragrances greeting you each morning as you sip your Cuban coffee. Enjoy the picture, it's just a fantasy---or is it?

Chapter 3

Where It All Started

To appreciate Key West architecturally, an understanding of its varied and colorful past is essential. Early settlers, as well as subsequent immigrants, left their marks on the city, while its natural isolation may have helped preserve a unique heritage.

KEY WEST, FLA.
1884

Not a lot is known about the first residents of Key West, who may have arrived as early as 7000 BC. Various groups of hunter/gatherer peoples continued to inhabit the island that Commodore Porter would describe as "covered with a thick growth of woods and filled with deer and other game." Ponce de Leon in his search for the fountain of youth became the first European to visit the Florida Keys, which he named Los Martieres in 1513. Permanent settlement of Key West, however,

would have to wait another 200 years. Some think that Ponce de Leon referred to the westernmost island in the southern archipelago as Cayo Oeste (Spanish for "West Key") and this was later corrupted to Cayo Hueso (Spanish for "Bone Island") as it is known to this day by its Latin neighbors. Another school of thought believes the name, Cayo Hueso, was given by Spanish visitors in the early 1700s when they discovered beaches littered with bones from battles between

Key West in 1855. Shipbuilding and repair was an important industry of the period.

Indian tribes. Present-day residents seem content with either designation.

Some of Key West's earliest seafaring residents were Indians who, in the 1700s, were crossing the turbulent Florida Straits in dugout canoes to trade with the Spanish. In 1763, when Florida was ceded to England, the Spanish relocated the last 80 Calusa Indian families to Cuba. Key West did not, however, remain unoccupied for long. Each year a fishing fleet of some 30 Cuban boats worked the productive waters around Key West, and Bahamian vessels began to appear as well. Florida, which had remained a de facto Spanish territory, was officially returned to Spain after 20 years but then became a United States territory in 1821.

Shortly before this transfer, the island of Key West was sold to John W. Simonton of Mobile for $2000 by the Spanish soldier, Juan Pablo Salas, the beneficiary of a land grant from the monarchy. Simonton acquired three partners; Pardon C. Green, John Whitehead and John W. C. Fleming, in what would become the first Florida land development. The city of Key West was

designed and mapped, and today's visitors will recognize the names of these city fathers assigned to four of its prominent streets.

While Bahamian vessels had been visiting the Keys for many years, the first permanent arrivals began in the 1830s. The ranks of settlers in the Bahamas had swelled due to the migration of Loyalists after the United States' War of Independence. While some tried unsuccessfully to establish plantation life on the thin-soiled Bahama islands, all eventually made their livelihood from the sea. The new Key West residents who came from the principal Bahamian settlements of Nassau and New Plymouth brought with them the name "Conch," from their appetite for the Queen Conch shellfish so abundant in Bahamian and Keys waters. They also brought much more: their skills at farming the sea for fish, turtle and sponge. A knowledge of shipbuilding and memories of northeastern seaport communities would also have an immediate and long lasting impact on the tiny village of Key West.

During the next few decades, Key West would

Key West's famous Duval Street in 1900, looking from the Gulf of Mexico to the Atlantic. The street was named after William Pope duVal, first governor of the Florida territory.

10

New Plymouth: A Beginning in the Abacos

A tiny settlement in the Abaco Islands of the Bahamas, New Plymouth has a special relationship with Key West. Citizens of these communities share a heritage, a similar island environment and many of the same surnames. The 500 or so residents of New Plymouth trace their roots to the Loyalists who chose to live in the Bahamas after the American Revolutionary War. From there, the migration led to Key West with some settlers even transporting their houses. Today, the two towns are joined as sister cities and proudly fly each others flags.

Walking up the narrow lanes from New Plymouth's harbor there is a vague feeling of familiarity. Wood frame houses in pastel colors are decorated with gingerbread, and the lots they occupy, tiny by American standards, are outlined by picket fences. On an island only 3.5 by 1.5 miles, land must be conserved.

Beneath the homes, cisterns were and still are used to store rain water collected by steeply-pitched roofs. In a few locations there is still evidence of the kitchen area, which the original settlers located in a separate structure to isolate the smoke and heat but, more importantly, to reduce the risk of fire.

Trees and plants contribute to the scene with the fiery red of the bougainvillea poking through and over white fences, and the burning orange of the Royal Poinciana tree spreading its umbrella over yards. Wandering through streets and shops, one encounters names with a familiar ring; Sawyer, Roberts, Albury, Lowe, Malone, Curry, Bethel and more.

Toward the center of town lies a beautiful sculpture garden where New Plymouth's early settlers are honored with a living memorial. Key West recently opened its own sculpture garden modeled after the New Plymouth concept. In a reversal of the migration trend, several Key West residents have been instrumental in the expansion of the Reef Relief organization from Key West to New Plymouth. The new office will occupy the old Capt. Roberts house, a two-story wood frame overlooking the neighborhood pictured above.

It feels good walking through this little town, whose residents greet you with an accent you can't quite identify. Without too much effort, one can imagine stepping back in history and strolling down a street called Duval in the newly settled community of Key West.

This imposing Eaton St. residence was built in 1885 by George Curry, son of William Curry, Florida's first millionaire. After the ravages of decades of neglect, the home is being returned to its former glory.

find itself at the crossroads of growing shipping activities and, with the treacherous reefs of the Florida Keys taking a deadly toll, a new industry, wreck salvage, brought an unprecedented era of prosperity. By 1850, Key West was the richest city per capita in the United States, with a wrecking fleet of 50 vessels. If business slowed, a couple of mules with lanterns strung on a rope between them could be walked along the beach to lure an unsuspecting ship closer to the reef. But an industry based on the misfortunes of others is always in jeopardy. A modern system of lighthouses eventually ended the wild days of wrecking.

Discontent in Cuba resulted in immigration and a new industry for Key West: cigar making. Tobacco was shipped to Key West from Cuba and, with an imported work force, factories were soon producing most of the cigars for the United States and world markets. From the 1850s through the next few decades, Key Westers enjoyed a period of cultural and economic boom The city was an important deepwater port and, in addition to a thriving cigar industry, a fleet of sponge boats now supplied the needs of the entire country. To celebrate its position as the wealthiest city in Florida, citizens dressed elegantly and enjoyed performances by European opera companies on tour. Geographically

International tensions due to the Spanish-Cuban-American War increased Key West's strategic importance. In this 1899 photo, the North Atlantic fleet lies at anchor off Key West.

April 23, 1982: Founding of the Conch Republic. "We seceded where others failed."

Tinajones

Evidence of Key West's colorful heritage can be found on every street. The earthenware jar above is a Cuban "tinajone" that has graced the yard of the Donkey Milk House longer than anyone can remember. Originally used to store water during periods of drought they are still a common sight in the old Cuban city of Camaguey. The huge jar above may have made its way here from that very city and been used as ballast on an early sailing vessel.

isolated but culturally linked to the great cities of Europe and the Americas, residents built grand homes reflecting these influences.

This high point in the status and wealth of Key West also marked the beginning of a slow decline. It was hoped that construction of the Flagler railroad linking the city with the mainland and the US's decision to build the Panama canal would buoy the prospects of the island. But, in fact, they did little to halt the decline. A devastating hurricane in 1935 destroyed the railroad and combined with a national depression to leave the 11,000 residents destitute.

Faced with the options of bankruptcy and evacuation, Key Westers chose to put a new face on their city and attempt to build a new prosperity on tourism. The overseas highway in 1938 made Key West accessible to middle America and, at the same time, the U. S. Navy became a significant contributor to the economic health of the island. The upswing was gaining momentum.

As the 1970s approached, however, Key West found itself again in a period of depression. The Navy was no longer a major contributor to the city's economic well being after a nationwide campaign to reduce defense spending, and a once-robust shrimping industry had begun a slow decline. City officials realized that renewed emphasis on tourism would be their best hope to avoid a devastating repeat of the 1930s.

A foundation had been laid in past decades and Key West had become a desirable retreat for a small elite corps of artists and writers, such as Ernest Hemingway and Tennessee Williams. The efforts would experience many obstacles but by the 1990s a new boom was in high gear. America had increasingly come to treasure its only bit of the tropics, and a colorful southernmost city with charming old homes.

Chapter 4

End of the Road
---or Center of the Map?

Near the southwest tip of this island sits a marina visited by ships of every flag. Until a recent name change, it was known as Lands End Marina, reflecting its location at the end of the road.

End of the road places are typically unique and colorful, and Key West is no exception. But is this an accurate point of view? Key West juts out into the Florida Straits where shipping traffic connects Gulf coast cities and Caribbean ports to the eastern United States and Europe. At a latitude of 24 degrees 34 minutes, it is our closest point to all the Caribbean nations and South America. If a Key Wester yearns for a little more culture, he could travel 180 miles north to the Florida mainland or he could look south. Just a short hop over the Straits lies a 500 year old culture where one can enjoy the ballet in the ornate Gran Teotro of Havana. A small fleet of modern day blockade runners quietly make this port on a regular basis.

To the east, lies the island nation of the Bahamas. More than a thousand islands, most of them uninhabited, make up one of the premier fishing, vacationing, and cruising grounds in the world. To the west, lie a variety of countries and interesting ports, many with historical links from the days when Key West was the richest city in Florida. Biloxi, Mobile, New Orleans, and Galveston are to the northwest.

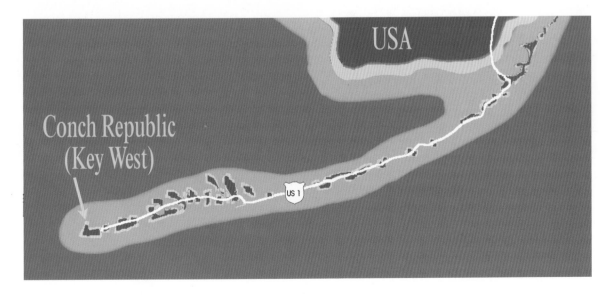

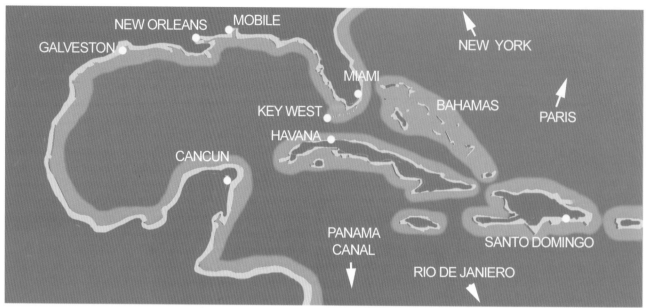

Key West---"The Center of the Map."

Further south, the Yucatan peninsula of Mexico juts out with its well known playgrounds of Cancun and Cosumel. Even further south you will find Central American nations such Honduras, Costa Rico, and Panama where Key Westers have migrated in the past.

So while our northern relatives may pity those of us living in our "end of the road" isolation, many Key Westers have a different view, a fascinating panorama view. They know that Key West is really the "Center of the Map".

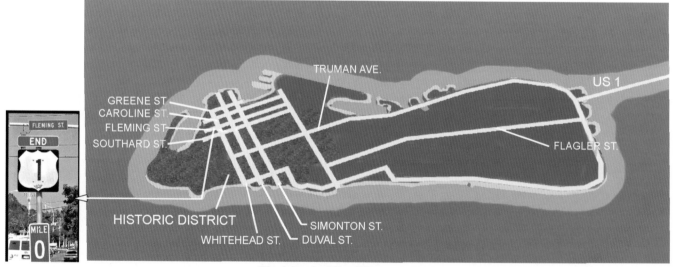

The Island of Key West

Chapter 5

A Rich Tradition in Architecture

Have you ever driven through a carefully planned community in which a few well-conceived house designs were repeated ad nauseam and felt claustrophobic over the endless sameness? Then you will love Key West. The historic district has been described as a patchwork whose many variations reflect its colorful 200-year history and the individuality of its citizens.

The Capt. John Lowe Jr. house has been described as Classical Revival with Bahamian influence. Prominent in the wrecker business, the Lowe family migrated to Key West from the Bahamas.

Upper levels are accessed by stairs located on porches of the Williams St. Bahama house.

Massive posts are joined by wooden pegs on this Eaton St. Bahama house.

Key West was settled by seafaring people who built their houses like they built their ships---to survive. In fact, actual shipwrights designed and built many of the early houses with craftsmanship and techniques now largely forgotten. Strip away interior wall paneling and you will see sturdy 4 x 4 (or larger) posts braced in the corners by diagonal timbers. The end of the diagonal piece will have been hand shaped into a tenon that fits with amazing precision into a mortise slot in the upright timber, and the two timbers held together with a wooden peg rather than nails. The wood of resinous Dade County pine is now so hard that a nail (or termite) can penetrate it only with great difficulty. This is the type of construction that characterized the homes of early wreckers.

Construction was not guided by architectural plans or constrained by building regulations. Using hand tools and available materials, shipwrights produced sturdy structures based on their memories from northern seaports and the practical considerations of tropical living. These were buildings that might flex in a high wind but would survive the many hurricanes that batter the island. Shipped or salvaged pine, mahogany or cypress may have been used. Raised first levels allowed added protection from hurricane winds and flooding, and permitted cooling ventilation during the steamy summer months. Cypress posts or limestone block piers to which sills were pinned were anchored into the island's limestone foundation and survive today. Higher up roof scuttles reproduced from ship designs provided ventilation to upper level rooms. Widow walks remembered from New England served a different purpose in Key West. They gave the wrecker captain a panoramic view of potential new clients on the distant encircling reefs.

The two side by side Bahama houses near the cor-

ner of Eaton and William Streets are representative of the early wrecking period. Part of the migration of Bahamians to Key West, they were disassembled in their original New Plymouth locations and brought to Key West by their owners, Capt. Richard Roberts and Capt. John Bartlum in 1847. These homes feature gen-

The carved pineapple, frequently seen atop posts, is a sign of prosperity and welcome.

This Victorian mansion is located at the corner of Fleming and Elizabeth, next to its identical twin. The homes were built in 1873 by L. E. Pierce for his two daughters. Its present, renovated state is courtesy of composer-lyricist Jerry Herman (*Mame, Hello Dolly*) and subsequent owners of the mansion.

erous porches and verandas, wide beaded-edge siding and exterior staircases. The deep porches and louvered doors and windows were all designed for comfortable living in a tropical environment.

With a growing wealth from the wrecking and shipping business, a richer, more sophisticated architecture began to emerge. Cut off from the mainland, the homes of Key West reflected influences from every point on the compass. Long eaves, ornate trellises, Gothic revival gables, ballusters and Greek revival columns were adopted and represented the fashion of the day in New England, New Orleans and the West

Indies among others.

Relocation of the cigar industry to Key West brought yet another wave of prosperity and construction. Wealthy Cubans constructed some of the great houses of Key West for their own use, and also were responsible for the proliferation of shotgun houses for their workers. This small, economical design was copied from similar structures found throughout the Gulf coast states.

This beautiful Queen Anne never fails to turn heads on Southard Street. If the octagonal turret, many porches and galleries, and gingerbread icing are not sufficient, a well-manicured garden with a Royal Poinciana centerpiece completes the visual banquet.

While it is true that the architecture of Key West is a unique patchwork reflecting the many influences that reached her shores, there is a certain homogeneity beneath the icing of balustrade and gingerbread. From the earliest period, land was a precious commodity, and Key West was no place for spacious expanses of lawn. Deep, narrow lots were the norm, and these did not allow generous side clearance. And, of course, little provision was made for the automobile on an island where travel was by boat or on foot. Possibly fear of Indian attack or protection from the elements also contributed to tight clustering of structures.

Certain basic designs became quite popular and were repeated throughout the city. Balustrades and gingerbread during the latter phases of construction of the historic district became factory produced and available in great quantity and variation. Nevertheless, through the loving attention of multiple owners, even the repeated designs have taken on an appealing uniqueness.

Today the architecture of Key West is one of the most significant attractions for a huge number of yearly visitors. But it is far more. Its more than 2000 homes are a living record of America's residential building traditions as well as a monument to a unique and colorful part of our history.

This Francis Street home is a perfect example of how humble shotguns have been turned into very appealing residences through decorative additions to the house and property.

This elaborate, well-preserved home on the corner of Fleming and Elizabeth streets has been classified as a Queen Anne style of Victorian architecture. It was built nearly 115 years ago on Duval street at the present location of the Kress building by John Sawyer. Later, using a rolling platform pulled by teams of mules, it was moved to its present location where the Navarro family became its new owners. Most Key West homes have wall coverings of board which can survive the strain and shifting from hurricane-force winds. The Sawyer-Navarro home, however, became the first house in the city to have its high-ceilinged rooms finished in plaster.

This Eaton Street landmark was first owned by Bineto Alfonso, then Antonio Diaz y Carrasco, Cuban consul to the United States. The ship's wheel gingerbread (at the top left) is said to have been carved in Cuba.

Row of Shotgun houses on Truman Street, near Duval.

This charming one and one-half style house received the loving attention of three successive renovation-minded owners during the period I lived in the neighborhood. Rear additions and a beautiful pool patio transformed a plain dwelling into a pleasant, comfortable Key West getaway.

A modest residence tastefully embellished by Classic Revival window/door trim elements and pleasing exterior colors.

This cottage, outlined by a 3-toot high picket fence and partially obscured by gumbo limbo, palm and mango trees, was the residence of America's greatest playwright, Tennessee Williams, between 1949 and 1983. The original framing was joined by wooden pegs.

The 120-year old structure was moved to the "outskirts" of town from its original Bahama St. location. The home contains a one-room studio where the author of "A Street Car Named Desire" and "Cat on a Hot Tin Roof" wrote.

24

The clean, trim lines of this beautifully restored Elizabeth St. residence illustrate the Classical Revival temple style very well. Note the incised porch and gallery beneath the attic level portico.

This stately temple with attached front porch sits on a Key West-size lot in the Meadows, a small neighborhood at the northeast edge of Old Town.

The ship's figurehead makes an interesting adornment for this Meadows home, and is a reminder of Key West's seafaring past.

One of the most embellished homes in the Historic district, the pink Gingerbread House is a favorite with visitors and Key West book writers. The home was built in 1870 by Benjamin Baker whose family emigrated from the Bahamas and introduced pineapple cultivation to the Keys. In addition to the lacy Gothic revival gingerbread trim, note the mid-height capitals on the six columns and the Italianate-style brackets under the roof eaves.

The Eyebrow style pictured in these examples (above and below) is a Key West original. It takes its name from the appearance of partially-hooded upper windows, as seen from the street side.

The Southernmost House is one of the most stunning Queen Annes on the island and the most photographed. It was built in 1896 at a cost of $250,000 and has had a distinguished and colorful ownership. Its rambling high- ceiling halls and prominent turret are fondly remembered by many Key West visitors and have entertained presidents and other dignitaries through the years.

Architectural Styles During Key West's Historical Period

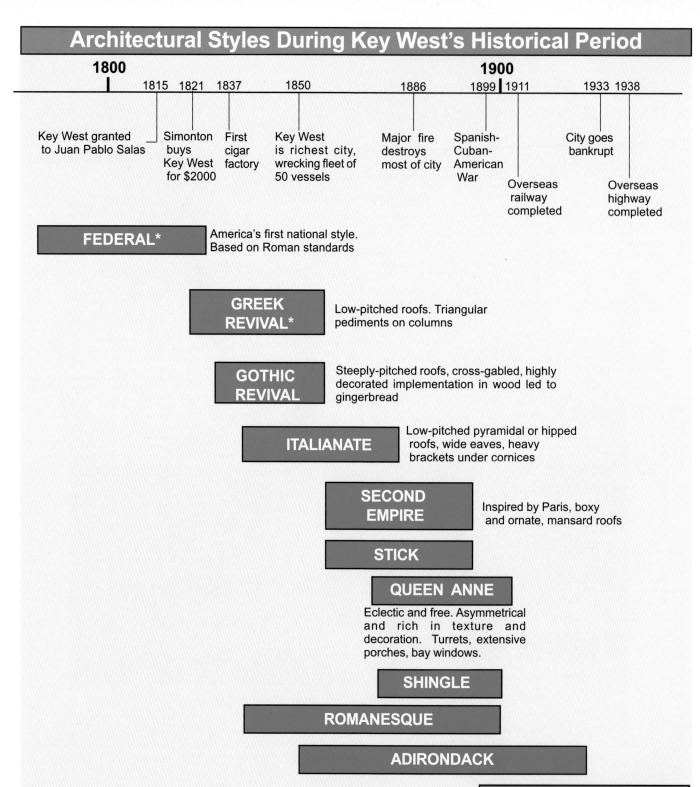

1800

1815 1821 1837 1850 1886 1899 1911 1933 1938

1900

Key West granted to Juan Pablo Salas

Simonton buys Key West for $2000

First cigar factory

Key West is richest city, wrecking fleet of 50 vessels

Major fire destroys most of city

Spanish-Cuban-American War

Overseas railway completed

City goes bankrupt

Overseas highway completed

FEDERAL* — America's first national style. Based on Roman standards

GREEK REVIVAL* — Low-pitched roofs. Triangular pediments on columns

GOTHIC REVIVAL — Steeply-pitched roofs, cross-gabled, highly decorated implementation in wood led to gingerbread

ITALIANATE — Low-pitched pyramidal or hipped roofs, wide eaves, heavy brackets under cornices

SECOND EMPIRE — Inspired by Paris, boxy and ornate, mansard roofs

STICK

QUEEN ANNE — Eclectic and free. Asymmetrical and rich in texture and decoration. Turrets, extensive porches, bay windows.

SHINGLE

ROMANESQUE

ADIRONDACK

NEO-CLASSICAL REVIVAL* — Italian Renaissance - Beaux Arts - Neoclassical Colonial Revival - French Revival - Spanish Revival - Tudor Revival

*The reader may experience some confusion over various uses of the term Classical Revival. Between 1770 and 1850 an interest in the classic Greek and Roman form has been referred to as Early Classical Revival. After a several-decade hiatus, a renewed interest emerged as the Neo-Classical Revival.

NEW AMERICAN VISIONS — Prairie school, Craftsman, Frank Lloyd Wright et al.

Chapter 6

Conch House Features

The history and photographs of Conch houses are fascinating, but now it's time to roll up our sleeves, lift roofs, open up walls and peer under crawlspaces

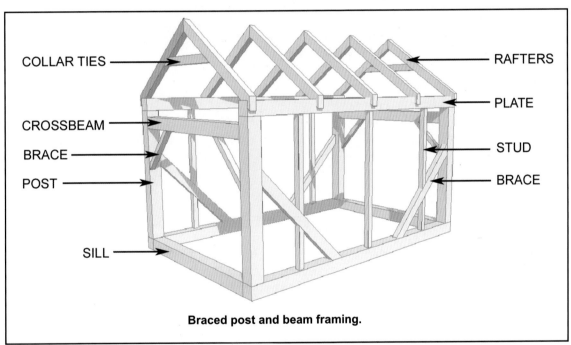

COLLAR TIES
RAFTERS
PLATE
CROSSBEAM
BRACE
POST
STUD
BRACE
SILL

Braced post and beam framing.

Many characteristics of Old Town homes have been thoroughly documented by the Historic Architectural Review Committee (HARC) in order to educate and preserve our heritage. Written material is available on request from their office on Simonton St.

Construction and Framing:
The Inside Story

Key West houses reflect a transition period in American homebuilding. Early houses in the colonial northeast were based on a method known as "post and beam" construction. Our virgin forests contained an abundance of long, straight timbers for building material, and these could be felled and shaped at the building site. Structural integrity was provided by a frame of upright posts set on bottom sills with crossbeams, plates, and rafters completing the structure.

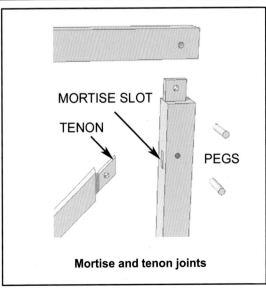

MORTISE SLOT
TENON
PEGS

Mortise and tenon joints

Mortise and tenon joints were carefully handcrafted so all elements would fit snugly and easily together as the building was raised. Nails were not yet available, so the joints were locked in place by wooden pegs or wedges. Since a square is not as rigid as a triangular shape, diagonal braces were employed to resist lateral stresses from wind loads and keep the structure square and plumb. These were attached to the uprights, sills, and plates with the same mortise-tenon joinery techniques. This basic braced frame is what gives these buildings an ability to withstand the elements and remain upright today. Studs placed interior to the frame were for attaching exterior panels that weatherproofed the building, rather than for load bearing reasons. It was this construction background that influenced Key West's earliest builders who mi-

Well-Preserved Interior of the Curry Mansion

A friend employed in the housing industry frequently bemoans the fact that so many houses continue to be built of wood. Concrete block, he feels, is the obvious choice. This is a personal decision, but as I think back to my house hunting days in Key West, I can't agree. I toured beautiful historic houses constructed from wood over one hundred years ago, but I also visited more recent concrete block structures. All presented some degree of maintenance challenge for the lucky buyer, but of a different nature, depending on the construction technique. The concrete block group sometimes had settling cracks in floor slabs and walls, and corroded metal windows needing attention. Blistering and bulging in walls indicated rusting reinforcing rods which needed to be chiseled out and replaced. While I thought my skill levels were up to replacing a few wooden siding boards or adding headers for new French doors, I was more intimidated when it came to masonry projects.

Wooden homes, which had withstood so many decades of hurricanes and termites, possessed another plus in my mind. They radiated a feeling of warmth and tradition, even in their sometimes distressed state. The walls and furniture of pine, cypress, oak, and mahogany that had once been living things displayed a richness in unique patterns that no other material can duplicate. Our forefathers must have been in awe of the vast virgin forests they found in America. They had left a world which had largely eliminated forests by the 13th century. They were forced to modify building designs to accommodate the shorter timber that was available, then turn to stone for building construction. But in America, huge straight timbers could again become the primary building material. Many of those timber frame houses and commercial buildings stand proudly today, testifying to the skill of their builders and the durability of wood.

grated here from the New England area by way of the Bahamas.

By the mid-1800's this braced frame construction was beginning to be replaced by stud framing employing mass-produced nails to attach butted joints. The reasons were the sawmill and westward expansion. Smaller, standardized wood elements could be mass produced in the new steam-driven mills and shipped great distances.

The house with nailed stud walls and plywood sheathing which performs the same function as the painstakingly crafted brace could be assembled quickly and with less skilled labor. This supported the needs of a rapidly expanding new country. Gradually, the balloon frame was superceded by the platform frame house. This construction approach allowed even greater efficiency during fabrication. Well-engineered struc-

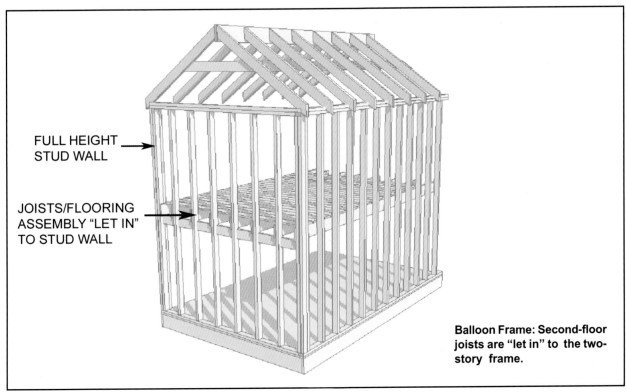

FULL HEIGHT STUD WALL

JOISTS/FLOORING ASSEMBLY "LET IN" TO STUD WALL

Balloon Frame: Second-floor joists are "let in" to the two-story frame.

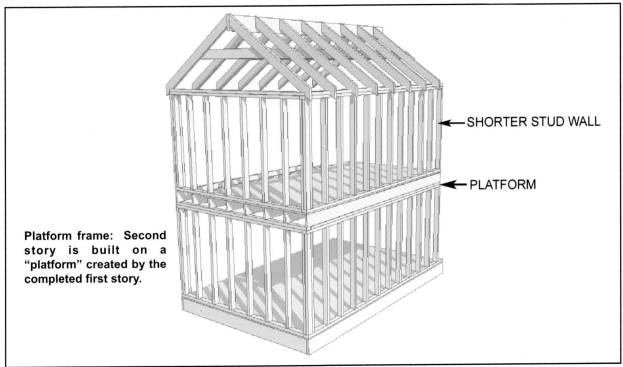

SHORTER STUD WALL

PLATFORM

Platform frame: Second story is built on a "platform" created by the completed first story.

tures using steel straps at key attachment points can withstand very high winds.

So the houses of Key West built from the early 1800's through the 1900's reflect the transitions in framing and construction described above. The older homes shipped here from the Bahamas used carefully crafted post and beam elements amenable to disassembly and reassembly. In later period homes, one continues to find large scale upright posts diagonally braced to floor sills with mortise-tenon joints but employing nails and interior load bearing studs reflecting newer construction approaches.

Foundations

On a low lying island, basements are usually not an option, and the homes of Key West are constructed on piers ranging from 1 to 4 feet. These were traditionally quarried limestone block or bricks. Cypress posts may have also been used to support some portion or all of the house. In a few instances, cypress or pine posts served as diagonal braces to oppose the huge lateral forces from the hurricane winds that sometimes battered the island.

Modern construction techniques use steel rein-

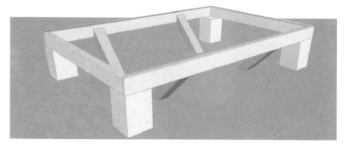

forced concrete pilings sunk three feet into bedrock. Protruding metal straps or bolts attach to wood beams and securely anchor a house to the island.

Lattice Infills

The areas between piers of the crawlspace have typically been filled with some type of lattice work. This allows the flow of air and (if necessary) flood waters, while providing a decorative enhancement. As illustrated, standard diagonal or box lattice, as well as vertical strip are traditional.

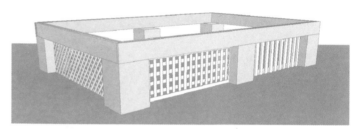

Surviving High Winds

In the past, many Key West homes had heavy cables attached to upper roof-wall corners and to buried pilings. With this "tethered" arrangement, roofs and, in fact, the entire house, were prevented from blowing away in hurricane force winds. Today, a well-engineered system of metal straps anchors roofs, walls and floors to steel-reinforced sunken pilings. With this less-obtrusive approach, the house can survive winds over 150 mph.

CABLE

Roofs

Homes in Key West's Old Town predominantly use metal roofs of two types. Most familiar is the V-crimp design which comes in the 2 foot-wide panels illustrated below. This is a relatively low cost roof, popular in many coastal areas. The panels overlap in two V-grooves on the sides and even work with very low pitch applications. They are generally purchased in stock lengths but procurable in custom lengths as well.

An older, more traditional, metal roof is based on the shingles shown below. These 9" by 12" panels interlock on assembly with surrounding panels and are nailed to the underlying roofing boards. Key West originally contained homes with more conventional wood-shingled roofs, but many were destroyed by the fire of 1886. In tightly clustered towns like Key West, fires were the most feared catastrophe, and almost all townspeople eventually switched to metal roofing when it became available.

Gutters were more important when homeowners' water supply depended on replenishing cisterns from afternoon rain showers. Early gutters were enclosed affairs built integral with the roof. The familiar half-round gutter was not introduced until well into the 20th century and is not considered truly historic.

Another feature of Old Town roofs were scuttles that allowed cooling breezes to circulate through second story areas. This feature was copied from ships by our early seafaring residents. Skylights of glass or Plexiglas would not appear until fairly recent times and today are confined to the rear of houses, where they are not visible from the street.

V-crimp metal roof

Metal shingle roof

Roof scuttles

Skylights

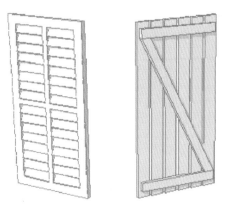

Side hinged louver and solid shutters

Bahama style top-hinged shutter.

Shutters - Not Just for Decoration

Shutters today define and beautify houses, and are protected from alteration on historic homes. Some homeowners might be tempted to attach them as non-functioning decorative elements. Anyone serious about preserving or replicating traditional houses should avoid this and attach operable shutters to windows. The reasons for shutters---security, shade, protection from tropical storm winds---are still valid today.

Shutters in Key West are usually of three types, as shown above. The choice is influenced by the function and style of house where they're applied.

Siding

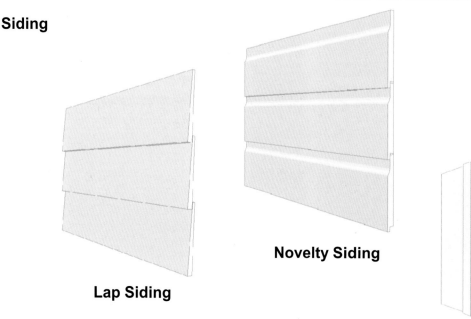

Novelty Siding

Lap Siding

Board and Batten Siding

Both vertical and horizontal siding boards can be seen on the houses of Old Town.

Many of the early shotguns used vertical 1x12's nailed to horizontal stringers with the seams covered by battens. Later homes, however, used larger standardized panels. The horizontal siding was of the lapped or the grooved type illustrated above. Usually 6-inch boards with a 5-inch exposure were employed.

Windows and Doors Define a Home

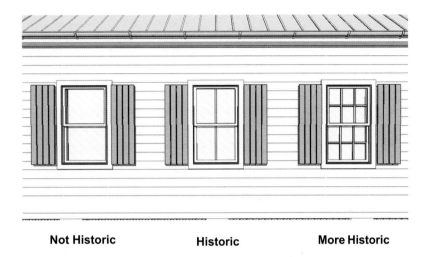

Not Historic   **Historic**   **More Historic**

On any house, windows and doors are among the most important architectural elements that distinguish a structure, and Key West's old homes display a variety of styles. Windows typically have high aspect ratio and are wooden and double-hung. The pane styles most common are 6-over-6 and 2-over-2. Some people theorize that 6-over-6 was popular because of difficulty in procuring larger glass sizes.

Door and windows trimmed in the Classical Revival style.

Entry doors for 19th century structures were the 4- or 6-panel variety. Later Greek Revival residences used 2-panel. In the great homes, paired doors and transoms and side lights were popular. French doors for front entry ways, as well as sliding doors, are not permitted in the Historic District.

Elaborate door and window surrounds are found on many homes, from small shotguns to large mansions. They are very effective in defining and distinguishing the structure even though they were certainly never employed by the cigar factory employee for his humble dwelling.

Interior Walls, Floors and Ceilings

A Key West cat ponders the beauty of Dade County pine

Key West houses were built before the introduction of plasterboard or other types of processed wall panels. While traditional plastered walls might have been found elsewhere, in Key West wood boards horizontally laid became the most common covering. In early homes, these were simply 1 x 4 boards butted together but later, tongue and groove gave a more refined appearance. This same type of covering was applied to ceilings, as well.

The material was frequently Dade County pine and it has survived very well over the many decades. Today, residents value this historic appearance and sometimes strip paint away to display the wood's warm, reddish tones. Sand blasting frequently achieved this in the past but is strongly discouraged now because of significant damage done to the wood. New and remodeled houses try to duplicate the original appearance by nailing historically precise boards to walls and intentionally allowing visible gaps and other anomalies of century-old walls.

Floors are tongue and groove oak or Dade County pine. Today, the original pine is emulated with yellow pine appropriately stained. A dark ebony stain sometimes adds an elegant, yet rustic and historic appearance. Frequently, reclaimed Dade County or heart pine flooring is used for a truly authentic result.

Porches and Miradors (Widow Walks, Captain's Walk)

Captain's walk (at the top) allows a 360-degree island view.

Key Westers love their treetop hideaways.

First- and second-story wraparound porches, as well as Captain's walks on roof tops, are the most identifiable and appealing features of Conch houses. Porches may be enclosed with gingerbread, square or turned-post ballustrades. Supporting posts are square, chamfered, round or have elaborately turned designs. Sometimes, two or more turned posts jointly support each corner on Classic Revival style houses.

Another unique feature frequently pointed out to visitors is the light green or blue paint on the undersides of porch roofs. Legend has it that this was a Bahamian custom to allow spirits to escape upward, as well as to prevent insects from nesting. The flooring on porches is almost exclusively tongue-and-groove, and painted a color which complements exterior walls and trim. In older homes especially, the floor has a very noticeable pitch for water drainage.

On an island surrounded by beauty, the rooftop Captain's walk is a pleasant addition. Its original purpose was to give the wrecker captain a view of ships that may have fallen in harm's way on the reefs seven miles distant. Today, a resident nestled at eye level with the treetops can sit back with his favorite sundowner drink and watch the sun dissolve into the distant horizon.

Key West Gingerbread---*Like Nothing Else You've Seen*

Ballusters, corner brackets and picket fences reflect tropical plants of the island, the owner's interests or advertise his profession.These porch ballusters graced a building active in the beverage trade during Prohibition. Notice how the cutout portions represent whiskey or wine bottles. In the brackets (near the top) a home owner expresses his love of the Queen Conch with an intricate abstract design representing the sea creature.

"Gingerbread" became an important element of the architectural style known as Carpenter Gothic. Fanciful trim designs of the Gothic period found expression in wood at the hands of American builders. In few other places were these architectural features expressed more richly than in Key West. More than a hundred distinct designs of ballusters and brackets are seen around the city. Some were factory-produced during the early nineteen hundreds but others are local cre-

ations that reflect the owner's imagination.

The many gingerbread designs of Key West are illustrated in template forms near the end of this book. The reader can reproduce a particular design or procure it from sources given in the chapter on products and services. Although they're not permitted in Key West's Historic area, gingerbread in highly maintainable plastic patterns are also available.

Fences Make an Artistic, Sometimes Humorous, Statement

The picket fences of Key West serve to delineate and decorate yards. In recent years, much more fencing has been added to obtain privacy for backyards. Much of this has been implemented along with foliage to achieve some tasteful isolation without a boxed in appearance. Old Town fences are regulated to be no more than 4 feet high around front yard, and side and back yards may be encircled with up to 6-foot fences. As in the case of gingerbread, Key Westers display considerable originality and charm in their designs. Some examples are shown below.

Exterior Colors

For the most part, houses in Key West were painted white with darker trim or, in some cases, were left unpainted. When exteriors were non-white, muted colors were typically employed, unlike the bright pastels found on some of our ancestors' homes today in the Bahamas The following color recommendations for Key West houses are reprinted from a Historical Architectural Review Commission publication.

Traditional Colors of Key West

Doors: White, black, red, dark green, natural finished wood
Exterior Siding or Body: White, pastels, light gray, beige, buff
Exterior Trim: White or off-white
Porch ceilings: Light aqua, light blue, white
Lattice: Dark green or white

Foundations: Natural or gray
Wood fences and gates: White
Iron fences and gates: Dark green or white
Masonry walls and fences: White, beige, gray
Railings, balusters and porches: White
Roofing, metal: Silver paint
Roofing, asphalt: Gray, white, black
Shutters: White, black, gray or dark green

Chapter 7

The Shotgun

The Shotgun house was so-named because, with all doors open, one could fire a shotgun from front to rear without hitting any part of the home.

To my knowledge this has not been tested in recent years but, perhaps, was a common occurence in the colorful past of Key West. The design was popularized in the mid-1800s, when the cigar industry moved from Cuba. Stogies were rolled, packaged and distributed around the world from Key West factories.

At its peak the industry employed more than 2,100 Cuban immigrants and, to house this workforce, hundreds of shotgun-style houses (located around the city today) were constructed. Originally simple, economic designs, they've been embellished over the years with fanciful facades and attached structures.

The exact origin of the shotgun house is uncertain, but similar dwellings are found throughout the southeastern United States. In its most basic form, the shotgun is a single story one-room-wide structure with a gable end facing front. Successive rooms line up front to rear, their doorways aligned and usually located to one side. Thus the economical use of interior space is carried nearly to extremes. Some shotguns employ a side hallway, however, providing greater pri-

vacy for rooms which then open onto it.

In the example shown here, an 18' x 36' structure is divided into a one bedroom/one bath interior arrangement with the living room in the front of the house and kitchen in the rear. A loft space is provided over the middle rooms, but living room and kitchen are opened up with vaulted ceilings.

Rear view

43

Shotgun Detail

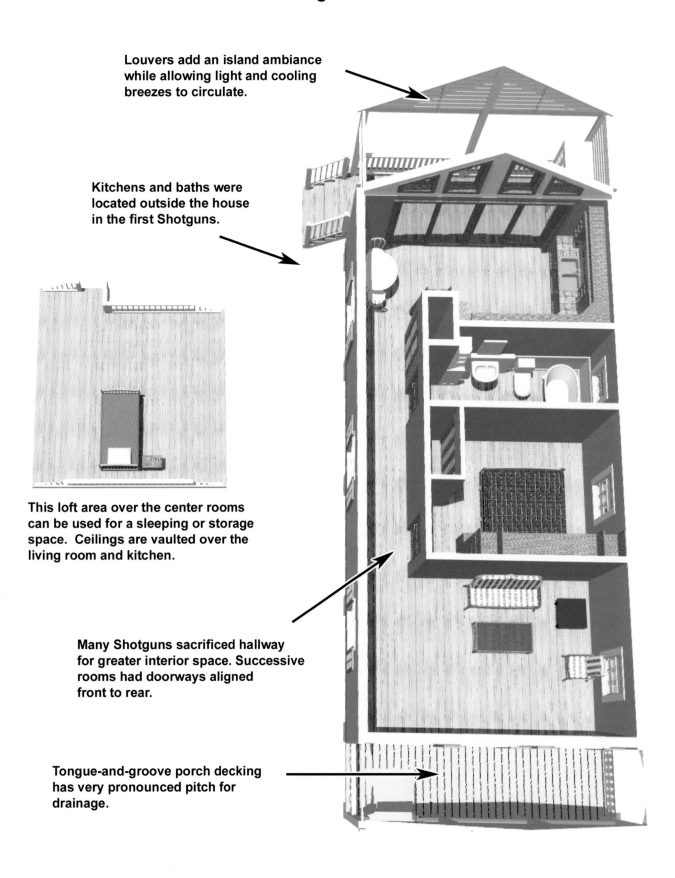

Louvers add an island ambiance while allowing light and cooling breezes to circulate.

Kitchens and baths were located outside the house in the first Shotguns.

This loft area over the center rooms can be used for a sleeping or storage space. Ceilings are vaulted over the living room and kitchen.

Many Shotguns sacrificed hallway for greater interior space. Successive rooms had doorways aligned front to rear.

Tongue-and-groove porch decking has very pronounced pitch for drainage.

SHOTGUN FLOOR PLAN

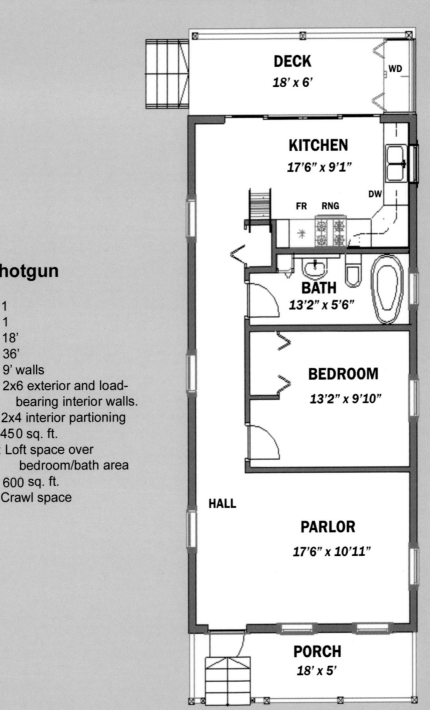

The Shotgun

Bedrooms: 1
Baths: 1
Width: 18'
Depth: 36'
Height: 9' walls
Framing: 2x6 exterior and load-
      bearing interior walls.
      2x4 interior partioning
First Floor: 450 sq. ft.
Second Floor: Loft space over
      bedroom/bath area
Living Space: 600 sq. ft.
Foundation: Crawl space

DECK
18' x 6'

WD

KITCHEN
17'6" x 9'1"

DW

FR   RNG

BATH
13'2" x 5'6"

BEDROOM
13'2" x 9'10"

HALL

PARLOR
17'6" x 10'11"

PORCH
18' x 5'

For detailed building plans, see information in Chapter 20.
Refer to "The Shotgun KW-001."

Chapter 8

The One and One-Half
This distinctive house style appears in many Key West neighborhoods

Although some call it the "One and One-Half," it is, in fact, a taller cousin of the Shotgun house. Additional living space is frequently attached later with one or more sawtooth-arranged gabled rooms (seen at the rear of the home). Through the years this structure has comfortably housed many Key West families.

The upper level has standup headroom near its center. With the space-expanding addition of gabled dormers, the result is an even more geometrically interesting upper level room. During recent renovation periods, creative new owners opened portions of the upper level of these style houses to provide vaulted ceilings for lower rooms.

The sawtooth appears as a clumsy afterthought to many visitors and new residents, but it served a serious purpose. The arrangement effectively captured rainwater and channeled it to cisterns. When one dis-

Rear view

covers the interior, it is surprising what clever renovation designs have been made possible by the unique ceiling angles.

Most One and One-Half houses in Key West have been tastefully embellished with gingerbread, door and window surrounds, shutters and balustrades on the incised porches. A picket fence enclosing a small front porch completes an appealing picture.

THE ONE AND ONE-HALF

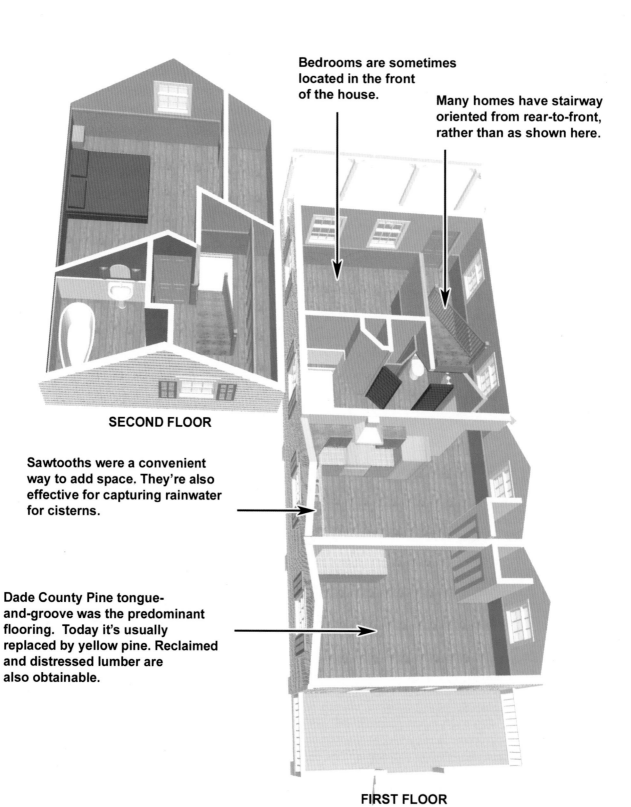

Bedrooms are sometimes located in the front of the house.

Many homes have stairway oriented from rear-to-front, rather than as shown here.

SECOND FLOOR

Sawtooths were a convenient way to add space. They're also effective for capturing rainwater for cisterns.

Dade County Pine tongue-and-groove was the predominant flooring. Today it's usually replaced by yellow pine. Reclaimed and distressed lumber are also obtainable.

FIRST FLOOR

(Houses shown in this book illustrate the major Key West styles.
Exterior and interior details do not represent any particular residence.)

48

ONE AND ONE-HALF WITH SAWTOOTHS
FLOOR PLAN

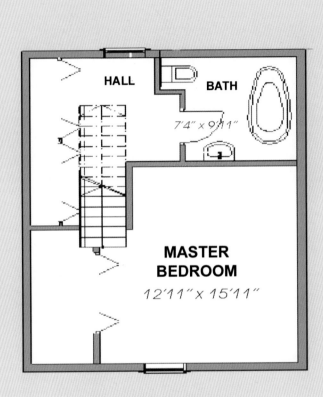

SECOND FLOOR

One and One-Half with Sawtooths

Bedrooms:	2
Baths:	2
Width:	18'
Depth:	40'
Height:	9' walls
First Floor:	720 sq. ft.
Second Floor:	360 sq. ft.
Living Space:	1080 sq. ft.
Framing:	2 x 6 exterior and load-bearing interior. 2 x 4 interior partitioning
Foundation:	Crawl space

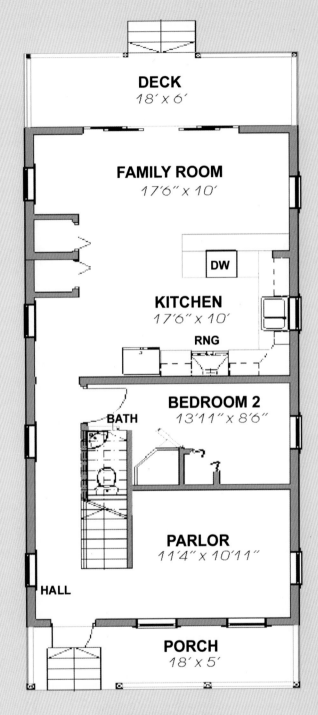

FIRST FLOOR

For detailed building plans, see information in Chapter 20.
Refer to "The One and One-Half KW-002."

Chapter 9

The Conch Cottage

This simple, traditional Conch house might be mistaken for many of America's small-town structures built after the turn of the last century if it weren't for the decorative gingerbread and interior construction.

The house used as a model for the design shown here was probably built between 1900 and 1925 and contains a heavily braced timber frame with mortise-tenon joinery.

The interior has a more comfortable and conventional layout than the previous two homes and provides space for two bedrooms with their own full baths. Most of the original cottage structures probably consisted only of the front portion of this example and the lower porch(s). Features like rear-gabled rooms, upper and lower decks and French doors came later. Key West's most famous resident of a cottage-style home was Tennessee Williams, whose home is pictured elsewhere.

Rear view

THE CONCH COTTAGE

Interesting tree-like decks abound, but were not part of the original Conch architecture.

Contrasting molding with different tones of a color above and below create a pleasing effect.

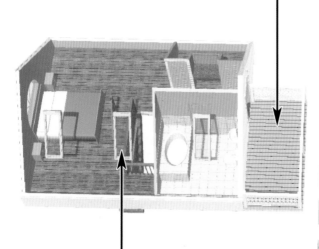

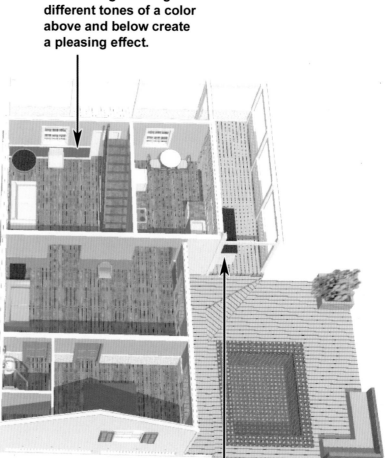

Skylights are generously used to brighten the upper level.

In tropical Key West, washer-dryers may be located on porches, but are tastefully enclosed

(Houses shown in this book illustrate the major Key West styles. Exterior
and interior details do not represent any particular residence.)

THE CONCH COTTAGE FLOOR PLAN

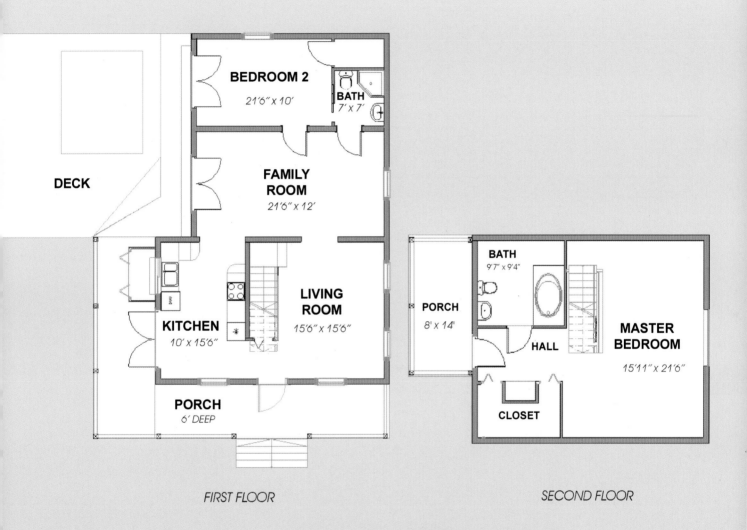

FIRST FLOOR

SECOND FLOOR

The Conch Cottage

Bedrooms: 2
Baths: 2
Width: 30'
Depth: 20'
Height: 9' ceilings
Framing: 2 x 6 exterior and load-bearing interior walls.
2 x 4 interior partitioning

First Floor: 868 sq. ft.
Second Floor: 548 sq. ft.
Living space: 1416 sq. ft.
Foundation: Crawl space

For detailed building plans see order information in Chapter 20.
Refer to "The Cottage KW-003."

Chapter 10

The Eyebrow

Unlike the other Conch houses that are, to some degree,
Key West adaptations of mainland designs, the Eyebrow
is an island original.

It contains much of the columned elegance of the Classic Revival temple, with a high-ceilinged front porch running the length of the house. Hooded upper windows, giving rise to the "Eyebrow" name, allow visibility, while remaining shaded from the tropical sun. Second-story space is generous in some cases, and, at the same time, interestingly constrained by the roof line angles.

In the rear, the roof line sometimes descends to nearly the height of the first floor. The interior is usually organized around a central hall which opens onto rooms on each side, and contains a staircase to second-floor sleeping areas.

Rear view

THE EYEBROW

Backyard cisterns are sometimes converted to small dip pools. The original excavation often provided the stone piers the house stood on.

FIRST FLOOR

SECOND FLOOR

Key West houses are historic from the street and innovative elsewhere

(Houses shown in this book illustrate the major Key West styles. Exterior and interior details do not represent any particular residence.)

THE EYEBROW FLOOR PLAN

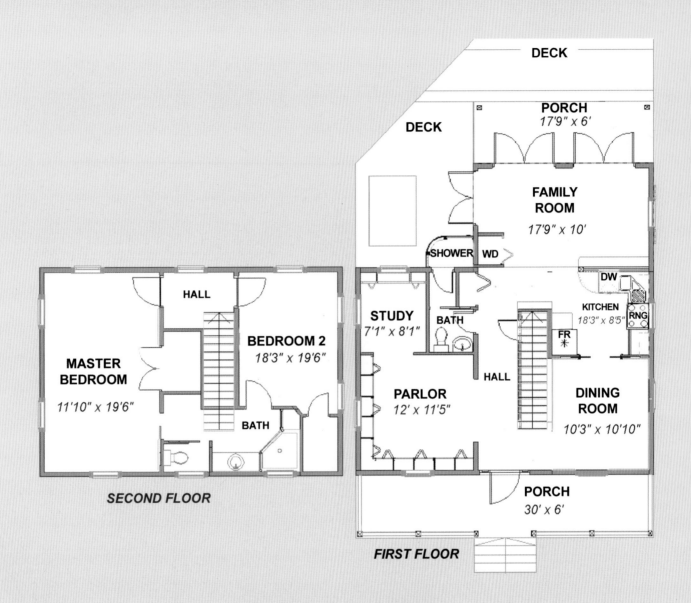

SECOND FLOOR

FIRST FLOOR

Eyebrow House Details

Bedrooms:	2	**Second Floor:**	600 sq. ft.
Baths:	2	**Living Space:**	1382 sq. ft.
Width:	30'	**Framing:**	2 x 6 exterior and
Depth:	20'		load-bearing interior walls
Height:	9' ceilings		2 x 4 interior partitioning
First Floor:	782 sq. ft.	**Foundation:**	Crawl space

For detailed building plans, see information in Chapter 20.
Refer to "The Eyebrow No. 004."

Chapter 11

The Classic Revival Temple

The stately temple design is one of the most recognizable architectural styles in Key West

During the early to mid-1800s, American architecture experienced a period known as Greek Revival. With concepts borrowed from Athen's fifth century BC Parthenon, designs for houses and public buildings were based on a rectangular two-story block, low-pitched roof, and formal columns symmetrically placed across the front-gabled entrance side. As the concept moved west and south from its northeastern origins, it evolved to meet local taste and practicalities. What survived became more commonly referred to as Classical Revival, and its influence even reached the isolated shores of Key West. Many examples of the two-story temple design can be seen in the commercial buildings that line Duval Street and on residential streets throughout Old Town.

The roof and attic-level portico extends over the upper gallery and first-floor porch. Although round classical-shaped columns are found, the majority of temple houses have rectangular posts framing the three or more front bays. Whether in their basic form or embellished with wrap-around verandas, octagonal side additions or other modifications, the temple house design is always an imposing, elegant structure.

Rear view

THE CLASSIC REVIVAL TEMPLE

In a latitude meant for outdoor enjoyment, many renovations open up the rear of the house. It gracefully transitions kitchen and family room with deck, patio and pool.

Horizontal Dade County Pine wall boards may be stripped to display the warmth of their reddish tones.

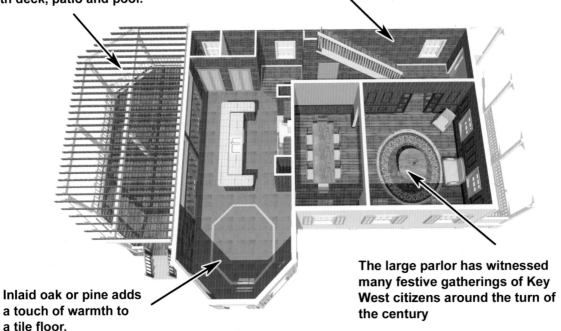

Inlaid oak or pine adds a touch of warmth to a tile floor.

The large parlor has witnessed many festive gatherings of Key West citizens around the turn of the century

FIRST FLOOR

Dressing area, with closets and vanity, is created with this semi-private arrangement

Second floor porch, known as a gallery, provides a pleasant sitting area off one of the bedrooms.

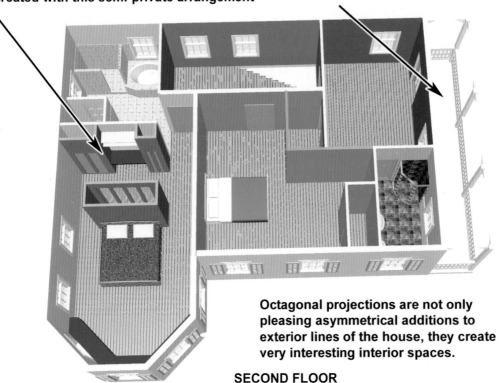

Octagonal projections are not only pleasing asymmetrical additions to exterior lines of the house, they create very interesting interior spaces.

SECOND FLOOR

(Houses shown in this book illustrate the major Key West styles. Exterior and interior details do not represent any particular residence.)

Classic Revival Temple Detail

Kitchen detail

Parlor detail

Master bath detail

THE CLASSIC REVIVAL TEMPLE FLOOR PLAN

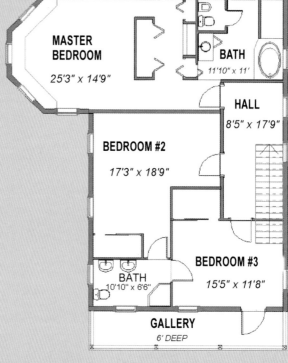

SECOND FLOOR

The Classic Revival Temple

Bedrooms: 3
Baths: 2-1/2
Width: 37'1"
Depth: 53'4"
Exterior Walls: 2 x 6 wd
First Floor: 1203 sq. ft.
Second Floor: 1203 sq. ft.
Third Floor: 849 sq. ft.
Living Space: 3255 sq. ft.
Foundation: Crawl space

For detailed building plans, see information in Chapter 20. Refer to "The Temple KW-005."

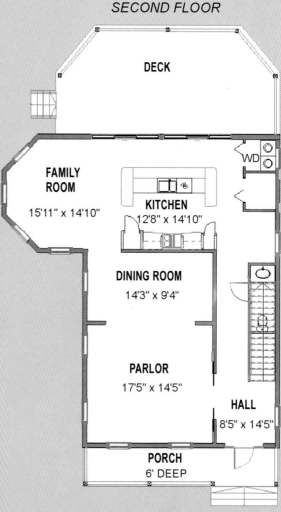

FIRST FLOOR

Chapter 12

The Conch Captain

No other great home conjures up such immediate images of Key West's seafaring past and tropical island heritage as the design we have designated "The Conch Captain." While exterior and interior layouts are generic, they represent older Key West structures built by Bahamian settlers. The generous wrap-around veranda and gallery were important living spaces to early Conchs, who enjoyed shaded outdoor living and cleverly designed their structures to capture cooling island breezes.

The captain's walk towering above treetop level gave the owner a panorama of the entire island and, of course, distant reefs. He could scan the horizon for approaching storms, overdue cargo, or ships in distress. More than most other houses, this design has stood the test of time and finds universal appeal today.

Rear view

THE CONCH CAPTAIN

Covered porches blend
smoothly with the
interior family room.

High gloss ebony stain
on wood floors yields an
elegant, tropical feel.

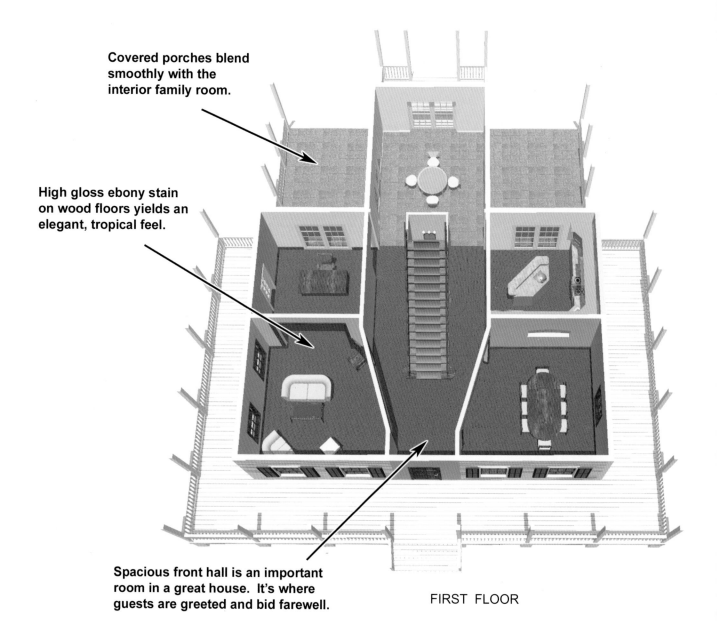

FIRST FLOOR

Spacious front hall is an important
room in a great house. It's where
guests are greeted and bid farewell.

Kitchen detail

(Houses shown in this book illustrate the major Key West styles. Exterior and interior
details do not represent any particular residence.)

64

THE CONCH CAPTAIN

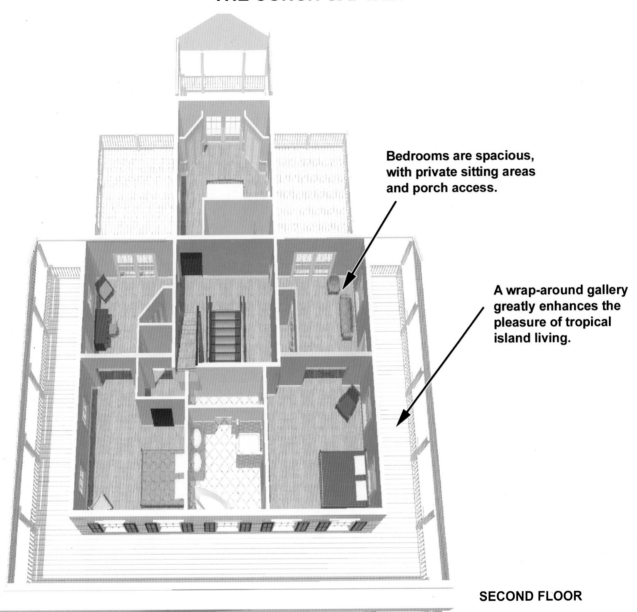

Bedrooms are spacious, with private sitting areas and porch access.

A wrap-around gallery greatly enhances the pleasure of tropical island living.

SECOND FLOOR

The Captain's Walk gave the wrecker captain, with spyglass in hand, a 360-degree view of surrounding reefs. In New England, this would be called the "Widow's Walk."

THIRD FLOOR

(Houses shown in this book illustrate the major Key West styles. Exterior and interior details do not represent any particular residence.)

THE CONCH CAPTAIN FLOOR PLAN

MIRADOR
13'5" x 11'5"

FOURTH FLOOR

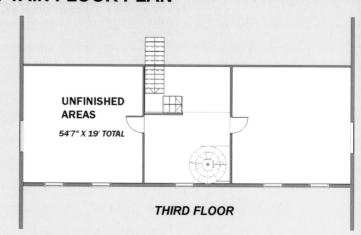

UNFINISHED AREAS
54'7" X 19' TOTAL

THIRD FLOOR

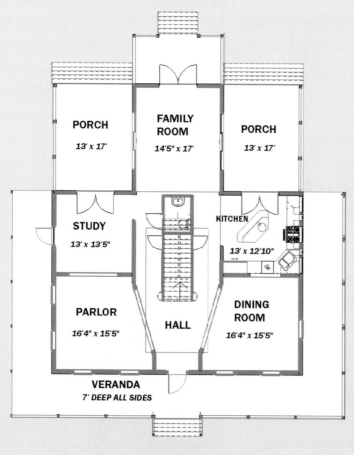

PORCH
13' x 17'

FAMILY ROOM
14'5" x 17'

PORCH
13' x 17'

STUDY
13' x 13'5"

KITCHEN
13' x 12'10"

PARLOR
16'4" x 15'5"

HALL

DINING ROOM
16'4" x 15'5"

VERANDA
7' DEEP ALL SIDES

FIRST FLOOR

DECK
13' x 17'

BEDROOM 3
14'5" x 17'

DECK
13' x 17'

SITTING ROOM
12'11" x 12'12"

SITTING ROOM
13' x 12'11"

BEDROOM 2
16'6" x 15'5"

BATH
8'9" x 9'10"

MASTER BEDROOM
15' x 15'5"

GALLERY
7' DEEP ALL SIDES

SECOND FLOOR

The Conch Captain

Bedrooms:	4	**First Floor:**	1444 sq. ft.
Baths:	3-1/2	**Second Floor:**	1444 sq. ft.
Width:	54'9"	**Third Floor:**	1032 sq. ft.
Depth:	60'8"	**Fourth Floor:**	153 sq. ft.
Height:	11' ceilings	**Living Space:**	4073 sq. ft.
Framing:	2 x 6 exterior and load-bearing interior walls. 2 x 4 interior partitioning	**Foundation:**	Crawl space

For detailed building plans, see information in Chapter 20.
Refer to "Classic House No. 006."

Chapter 13

The Mansion

The Mansion style represents
many of the great houses of Key West

Built by ships' captains or, more likely, a new class of prosperous merchants in the late 1800's, the Mansion represented a cultural coming of age for the community. Wrap-around veranda, large parlor opening from a richly wood-paneled entry hall and a formal dining room---all suggest images of a fascinating period. One imagines elegant social gatherings with flowing gowns, black suits, top hats and glasses raised to a new, prosperous era on the island. In varying forms these spacious, elegant homes never fail to capture the attention of passersby, and all have interesting pasts.

Rear view

THE MANSION

Ornate pocket doors of wood and etched glass separate parlor from hall and dining room.

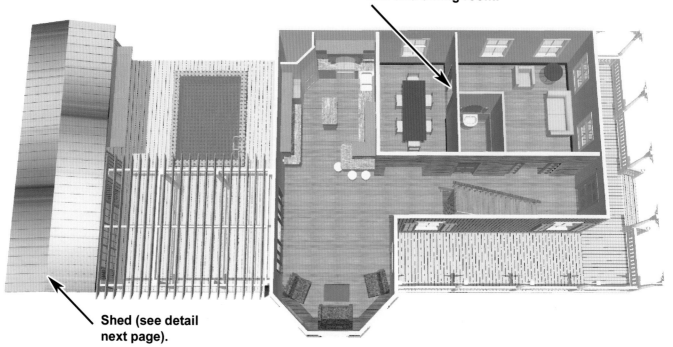

Shed (see detail next page).

FIRST FLOOR

Gallery access shared by two bedrooms.

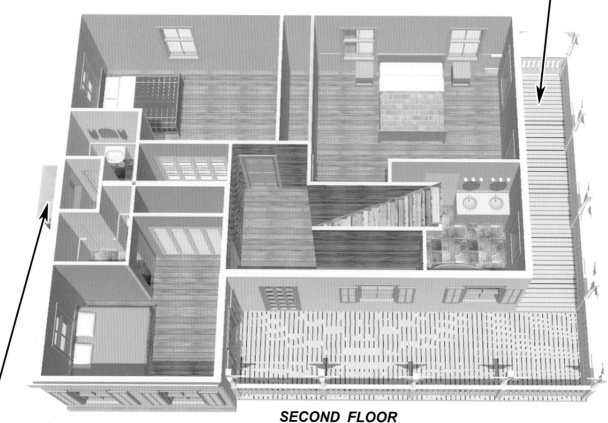

Shower area opened up with a bay window.

SECOND FLOOR

(Houses shown in this book illustrate the major Key West styles. Exterior and interior details do not represent any particular residence.)

THE MANSION: DETAIL

Kitchen

Shed is often remodeled to create more leisure space or guest quarters.

Bathroom

THE MANSION FLOOR PLAN

BEDROOMS OR STORAGE AREA

29'6" x 37'4"

Third Floor

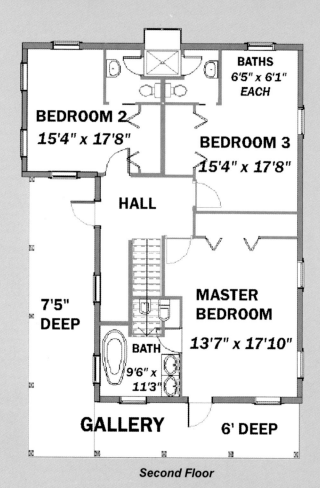

BATHS
6'5" x 6'1"
EACH

BEDROOM 2
15'4" x 17'8"

BEDROOM 3
15'4" x 17'8"

HALL

7'5"
DEEP

MASTER BEDROOM
13'7" x 17'10"

BATH
9'6" x 11'3"

GALLERY

6' DEEP

Second Floor

Mansion Details

Bedrooms: 3
Baths: 2-1/2
Width: 40'
Depth: 35'10"
Exterior Walls: 2 x 6
First Floor: 1034 sq. ft.
Second Floor: 1034 sq. ft.
Third Floor: 828 sq. ft.
Living Space: 2896 sq. ft.
Foundation: Crawl space

For detailed building plans, see information in Chapter 20.
Refer to "The Mansion KW-007."

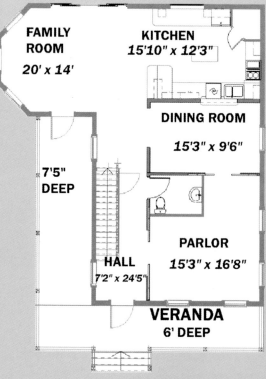

FAMILY ROOM
20' x 14'

KITCHEN
15'10" x 12'3"

DINING ROOM
15'3" x 9'6"

7'5"
DEEP

PARLOR
15'3" x 16'8"

HALL
7'2" x 24'5"

VERANDA
6' DEEP

First Floor

Chapter 14

The Queen Anne

In the latter half of the 1800s, America experienced a period of ornate design known as the Victorian age. During the last two decades of the period, an embellished version known as the Queen Anne gained popularity before falling from favor in the 1900s. These influences reached America's southernmost island and today, forty-four examples of the Queen Anne still stand.

The Queen Anne's highly asymmetrical floor plan and heavily decorated exterior are in striking contrast to the clean simplicity of other houses, such as the Classical Revival Temple. Today there is a renewed affection for this rambling, exuberant design, and owners find its interesting interior spaces create an elegant and enjoyable living environment.

THE QUEEN ANNE

The porch was an important living space before television and air conditioning. It provided shade and cooling, as well as a place to greet and socialize with neighbors.

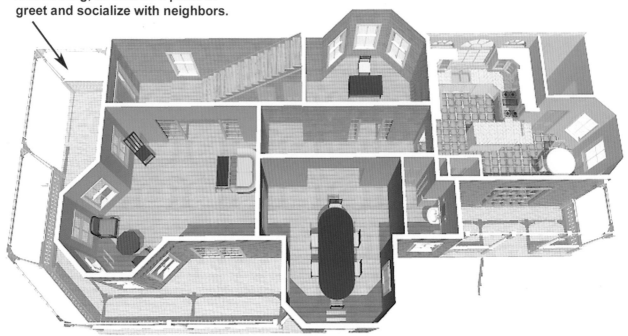

FIRST FLOOR

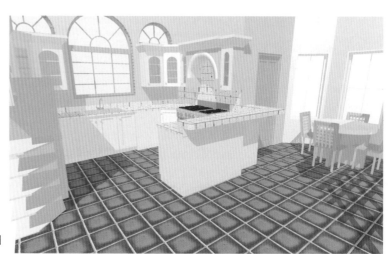

Kitchen detail

(Houses shown in this book illustrate the major Key West styles. Exterior
and interior details do not represent any particular residence.)

THE QUEEN ANNE

Spacious and ornate, the asymmetrical twists and turns of the Victorian create interesting, charming interior spaces.

Spiral staircase leads to general-purpose third floor space.

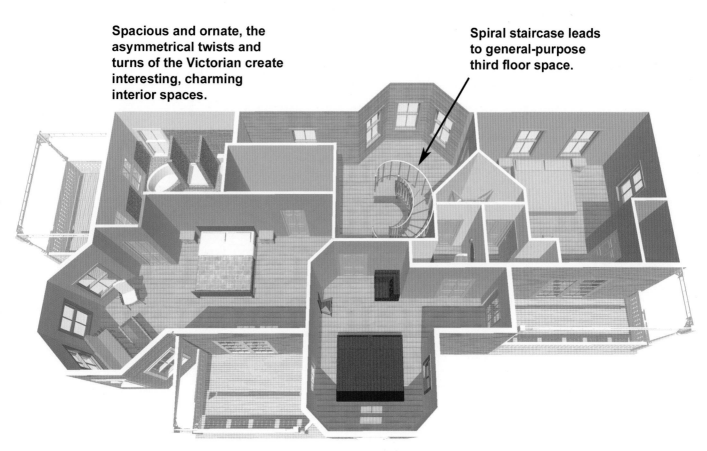

SECOND FLOOR

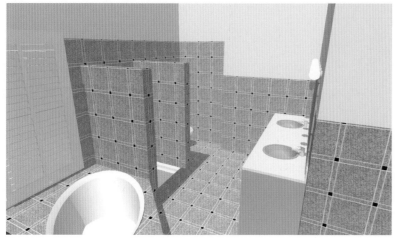

Master bath detail

THE QUEEN ANNE FLOOR PLAN

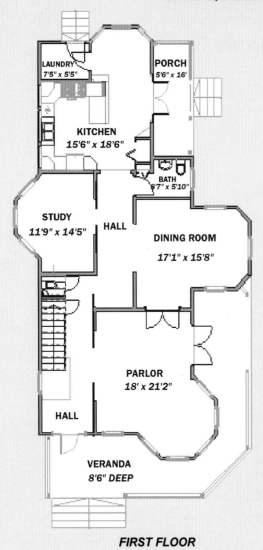

FIRST FLOOR

LAUNDRY
7'5" x 5'5"

PORCH
5'6" x 16'

KITCHEN
15'6" x 18'6"

BATH
6'7" x 5'10"

STUDY
11'9" x 14'5"

HALL

DINING ROOM
17'1" x 15'8"

PARLOR
18' x 21'2"

HALL

VERANDA
8'6" DEEP

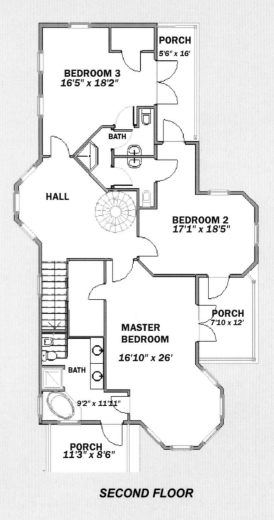

SECOND FLOOR

BEDROOM 3
16'5" x 18'2"

PORCH
5'6" x 16'

BATH

HALL

BEDROOM 2
17'1" x 18'5"

PORCH
7'10 x 12'

MASTER
BEDROOM
16'10" x 26'

BATH
9'2" x 11'11"

PORCH
11'3" x 8'6"

THE QUEEN ANNE VICTORIAN

Bedrooms: 4
Baths: 3
Width: 35'1"
Depth: 67'3"
Height: 10' ceilings
Framing: 2 x 6 exterior and
          load-bearing walls
First Floor: 1360 sq. ft.
Second Floor: 1345 sq. ft.
Third Floor: 1003 sq. ft.
Living Space: 3708 sq. ft.
Foundation: Crawl space

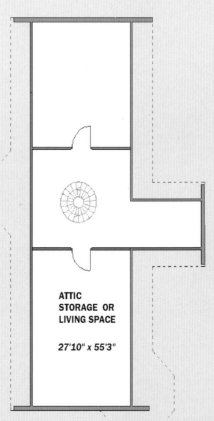

THIRD FLOOR

ATTIC
STORAGE OR
LIVING SPACE

27'10" x 55'3"

For detailed building plans, see information
in Chapter 20. Refer to
"The Queen Anne Victorian KW-008."

Chapter 15

The Bahama House

Ask a Conch about historical homes and chances are he will describe the two Bahama houses near the corner of Eaton and William Streets. None are more uniquely intertwined with early Key West history than these structures, disassembled in the Bahamian Abacos, and brought by schooner to their present locations.

Their first owners were Captains Richard Roberts and John Bartlum, both descendants of Loyalists who had moved to the Bahamas after the American Revolution. Beautifully maintained, these grand old homes give insights into Key West's earliest period and our seafaring ancestors who were migrating to this new, prosperous island.

Deep porches run the length of both houses behind massive square posts that extend from ground to roof. The Bartlum house on Eaton Street has a veranda that extends around its William Street side on both first and second floor levels. A trademark of Bahamian houses were stairways between levels located on porches to save interior space. Tall windows that begin just inches from floor level open the rooms to cooling breezes and light. Louvers added to doors and windows contribute to the distinctive island flavor.

THE BAHAMA HOUSE

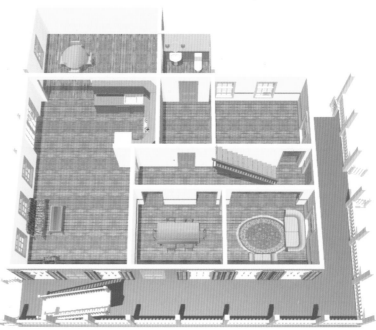

FIRST FLOOR

SECOND FLOOR

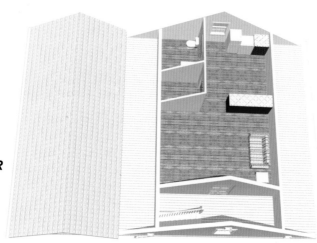

THIRD FLOOR

(Houses shown in this book illustrate the major Key
West styles. Exterior and interior details do not
represent any particular residence.)

THE BAHAMA FLOOR PLAN

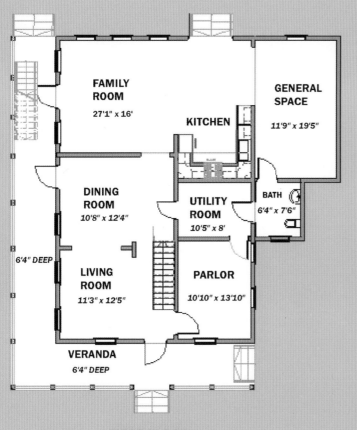

FIRST FLOOR

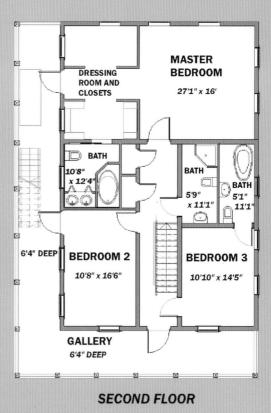

SECOND FLOOR

The Bahama

Bedrooms: 3
Baths: 4
Width: 34'4"
Depth: 48'4"
Height: 8' ceilings
Foundation: Crawl space
First Floor: 1472 sq. ft.
Second Floor: 1176 sq. ft.
Third Floor: 558 sq. ft.
Living Space: 3206 sq. ft.
Framing: 2 x 6 exterior and
load-bearing interior wall.
2 x 4 interior partitioning

THIRD FLOOR

For detailed building plans, see
information in Chapter 20.
Refer to "The Bahama KW-009."

Chapter 16

Contemporary with a Key West Flair

Homes in this chapter take inspiration from classic residences of Key West and retain much of the timeless charm and appeal of these structures. Interior architectural features, however, are thoroughly modern and comfortable in every respect. Whether you're considering a modest cottage or impressive three-story residence, you will find well-engineered building designs for new urban environments that are increasingly appealing to many Americans and spreading across coastal communities. These, and additional Key West- inspired home designs, can be found on the web site; **www.southerncoastaldesigns.com**

The Duval

The Duval, as viewed from the street, contains architectural elements of one of the most stately and unique Key West house styles, the Eyebrow. The two- story columned front facade is Classic Revival in origin but the metal roof, gingerbread brackets and ballustrade are unmistakable evidence of the southernmost roots of this home. Step through the front doorway and you are greeted with a skillfully designed, modern interior space featuring two bedrooms, clever loft study, great room under vaulted ceilings, and a highly functional kitchen layout. But the Duval is meant for outdoor living in coastal areas where views of the ocean can be savored. An upper gallery opens from the master bedroom and, downstairs, a multilevel deck contains covered and open spaces with outdoor bar and spa.

Rear view

THE DUVAL FLOOR PLAN

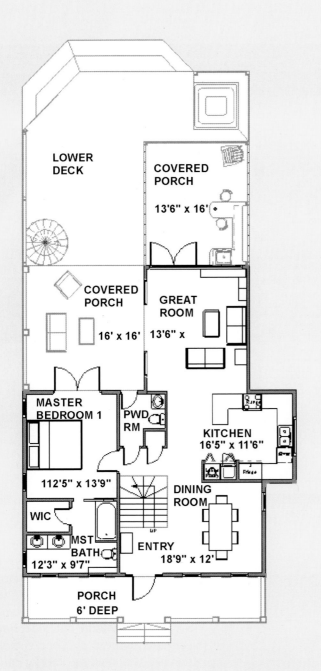

LOWER
DECK

COVERED
PORCH

13'6" x 16'

COVERED
PORCH

16' x 16'

GREAT
ROOM

13'6" x

MASTER
BEDROOM 1

PWD
RM

KITCHEN
16'5" x 11'6"

112'5" x 13'9"

WIC

DINING
ROOM

MST
BATH
12'3" x 9'7"

ENTRY
18'9" x 12'

PORCH
6' DEEP

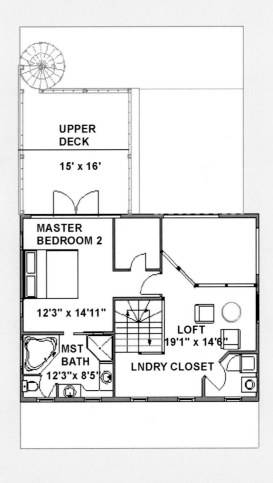

UPPER
DECK

15' x 16'

MASTER
BEDROOM 2

12'3" x 14'11"

MST
BATH
12'3"x 8'5"

LOFT
19'1" x 14'6"

LNDRY CLOSET

The Duval

Bedrooms: 2
Baths: 2-1/2
Width: 32'
Depth: 62'
Ceiling Height: 10'

First Floor: 1040 sq. ft.
Second Floor: 768 sq. ft.
Total Living Space: 2610 sq. ft.
Framing: 2 x 6 exterior walls
2 x 4 interior partitioning
Foundation: Crawl space

For detailed building plans,
see information in Chapter 20.
Refer to "The Duval KW-010."

The Marquesa

Rear view

The Marquesa is named after a small island group to the west of Cayo Hueso which held and protected the treasure of the Spanish galleon Atocha for four hundred years. This island home would be less a hidden treasure but rather one to be seen and admired by your visitors and friends. The modern interior provides large luxurious space for a single family, and the flexibility for shared usage, as well. A large great room on the second floor with two-story ceiling is the centerpiece of the house. A huge master bedroom, bath, loft sitting area and covered porch occupy the entire third floor. A staircase ascends to a covered widow's walk designed for spectacular views.

THE MARQUESA FLOOR PLAN

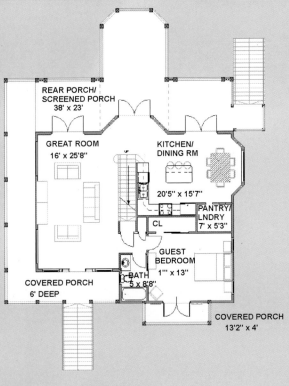

SECOND FLOOR

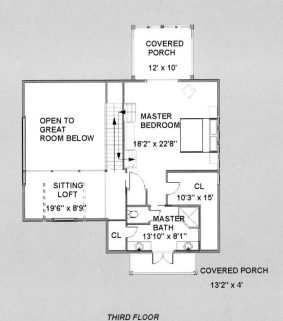

THIRD FLOOR

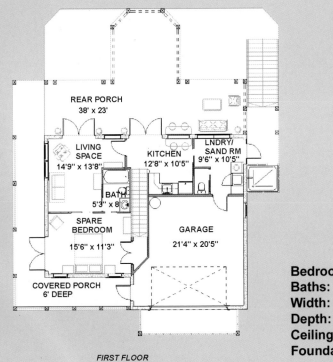

FIRST FLOOR

WIDOW'S WALK

The Marquesa

Bedrooms; 3
Baths: 3-1/2
Width: 44'
Depth: 55'
Ceiling Height: 10'
Foundation: Pilings/slab

First Floor: 675 sq. ft.
Second Floor: 1156 sq. ft.
Third Floor: 1120 sq. ft.
Total Living Space: 5469 sq. ft.
Framing: 2 x 4 exterior walls
2 x 4 interior partitions
(Poured concrete first floor)

For detailed building plans, see
information in Chapter 20.
Refer to "The Marquesa KW-011."

The Angela

This cottage with wrap-around porch is patterned after a building style seen in many Key West neighborhoods. In fact, one well-known resident, Phillip Burton, author, playwright, lecturer and father of Richard Burton, lived in a similar home from 1974 to 1995. The great room located in the front of the house is bright and cheerful, surrounded by windows and porch on three sides. A master bedroom and bath, very large by Key West cottage standards, is located in the rear and opens to the deck/pool area. Just off the pool is a sunroom whose wall of glass can be opened to change from an interior to an exterior space.

Rear view

THE ANGELA FLOOR PLAN

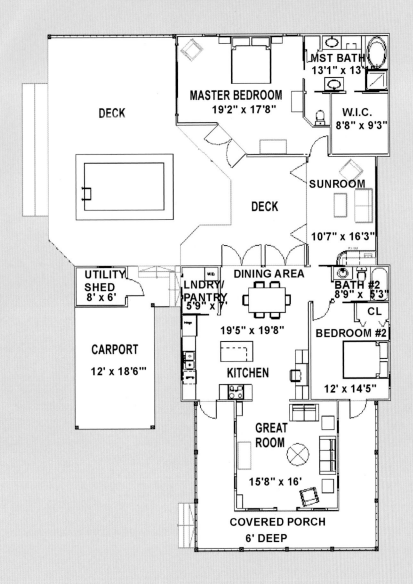

MST BATH
13'1" x 13'

MASTER BEDROOM
19'2" x 17'8"

DECK

W.I.C.
8'8" x 9'3"

SUNROOM
10'7" x 16'3"

DECK

UTILITY SHED
8' x 6'

LNDRY/PANTRY
5'9" x 7'

DINING AREA
19'5" x 19'8"

BATH #2
8'9" x 5'3"

CL

BEDROOM #2
12' x 14'5"

CARPORT
12' x 18'6"'

KITCHEN

GREAT ROOM
15'8" x 16'

COVERED PORCH
6' DEEP

The Angela

Bedrooms:	2	**Interior Space:**	1552 sq. ft.
Baths:	2	**Total Living Space:**	1819 sq. ft.
Width:	32'	**Framing:**	2 x 6 exterior walls
Depth:	76'		2 x 4 interior partitions
Ceiling Height:	10'	**Foundation:**	Crawl space

For detailed building plans, see
information in Chapter 20.
Refer to "The Angela KW-012."

The Southard

The clean, elegant lines of the Southard combine a solid, traditional first impression with a modern comfortable interior layout. The three-bay symmetrical front facade is borrowed from the temple design found in many Key West neighborhoods. Inside, the layout is decidedly 21st century. The visitor is greeted with a small parlor area to one side and staircase to upper levels on the right. A kitchen area has an easy, economical layout with a separate dining area. Both an indoor and outdoor great room are located in the rear of the house. The outdoor covered room has a large table-level bar area, completely open and flowing into the kitchen. In addition to the first-level guest bedroom, two more bedrooms are located upstairs. A second upstairs laundry is a convenience increasingly appreciated by modern home buyers, as is the shared loft study which opens to the front gallery. The large master bedroom has a private French door access to the rear gallery.

The Southard

Rear view.

Detail, showing outdoor covered room.

THE SOUTHARD FLOOR PLAN

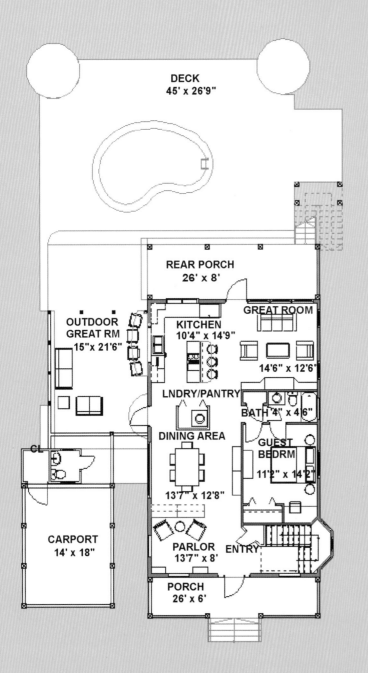

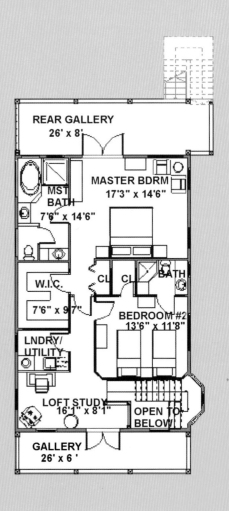

The Southard

Bedrooms: 3
Baths: 3-1/2
Width: 26'
Depth: 54'
Ceiling Height: 10'
Foundation: Crawl space

First Floor: 1053 sq. ft.
Second Floor: 1053 sq. ft.
Living Space: 3192 sq. ft.
Framing: 2 x 6 exterior walls
2 x 4 interior partitions

For detailed building plans, see
information in Chapter 20.
Refer to "The Southard KW-013."

The Lighthouse

This home's exterior lines were inspired by the famous old lighthouse keeper's home on Whitehead St. in Key West. The encircling porch provides shade for outdoor living in a coastal setting with panoramic views. A large enclosed observation/leisure room sits astride the house and features a wet bar and disappearing wall that opens interior space to the rear upper deck. Ten-foot ceilings of the main part of the house further contribute to its charming, historical feel but in every other respect, interior space is designed for modern living.

Rear view

THE LIGHTHOUSE FLOOR PLAN

SECOND FLOOR

UPPER DECK
18' x 16'

OBSERVATION ROOM
18' x 18'

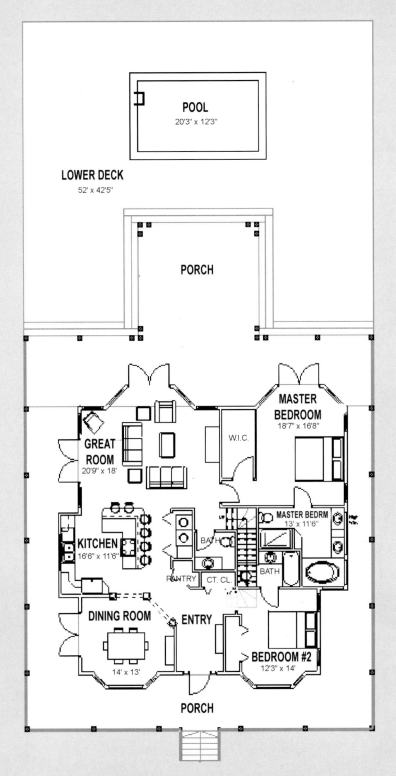

POOL
20'3" x 12'3"

LOWER DECK
52' x 42'5"

PORCH

MASTER BEDROOM
18'7" x 16'8"

W.I.C.

GREAT ROOM
20'9" x 18'

KITCHEN
16'6" x 11'6"

MASTER BEDRM
13' x 11'6"

BATH

PANTRY   CT. CL.   BATH

DINING ROOM
14' x 13'

ENTRY

BEDROOM #2
12'3" x 14'

PORCH

FIRST FLOOR

The Lighthouse

Bedrooms: 2
Baths: 2-1/2
Width: 52'
Depth: 74'
Ceiling Height: 10' first floor
9' second floor
First Floor: 1568 sq. ft.
Second Floor: 324 sq. ft.
Living Space: 1892 sq. ft.
Framing: 2 x 6 exterior walls
2 x 4 interior partitions
Foundation: Crawl space

For detailed building plans, see
information in Chapter 20.
Refer to "The Lighthouse KW-014."

The Olivia

If you have a modest-sized lot with a fantastic view, the Olivia could be a perfect choice for a vacation or retirement home. The charm and Key West pedigree of this architectural classic will be widely admired, and you will enjoy a layout designed for southern coastal living. Each of the two bedrooms on the second floor has access to its own private porch, providing outdoor sitting rooms with three- way views. The spacious great room and efficiently laid-out kitchen flow smoothly to the large L-shaped rear porch.

Rear view

THE OLIVIA FLOOR PLAN

FIRST FLOOR

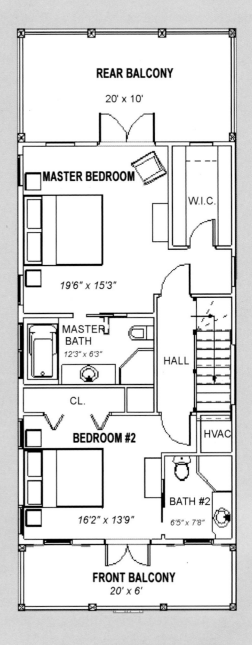

SECOND FLOOR

The Olivia

Bedrooms: 2

Baths: 2-1/2

Width: 20'

Depth: 52'

Ceiling Height: 10' first floor

9' second floor

First Floor: 738 sq. ft.

Second Floor: 864 sq. ft.

Living Space: 1602 sq. ft.

Framing: 2 x 6 exterior walls

2 x 4 interior partitions

Foundation: crawl space

For detailed building plans, see information in Chapter 20. Refer to "The Olivia KW-015".

Chapter 17

Gardens and Flora of Key West

Next to imaginative interiors, the most striking improvements to Key West homes in recent years have been well-conceived, beautifully implemented patios, yards and gardens. From the days of the sailing captains, Key West could boast a large variety of exotic plants, but this tradition has been greatly expanded by today's outdoor-minded citizens. Swimming pools are not just rectangular concrete affairs, but tropical oases, with waterfalls and hanging fruit within arm's reach. Stone or brick walkways meander through a colorful variety of flora, past aviaries, fish ponds and possibly leading to hidden meditation gardens.

Two impressive examples of Key West's beautiful outdoor creations are illustrated on the following pages. Also in this section are complete tables of outdoor plants and trees found in the city and neighboring keys. USDA zones showing where these plants flourish are identified for readers anxious to recreate the beauty of Key West in other locations.

The Spanish Limes

Like much of the plant life in Key West the Spanish Lime tree (mamoncilla) is a transplant. It probably arrived via Havana and its fruit remains a favorite with young Cuban children. The name "lime" is a bit misleading. You wouldn't want to use this lime in your Daquiris or Key Lime pies, but its plum-size fruit provides a pleasant taste diversion. It is mainly eaten raw but can be made into a pie filling or jelly. While Spanish lime can be found part of the way up both coasts of Florida, it is plentiful only in Key West.

The impressive giant to the left extends its  canopy over three Old Town homes, providing shade in the summer and attention-getting thumps as its fruit lands on tin roofs in August.

The Medicine Garden is a hidden place created for personal contemplation amid the beauty of tropical flora and the silence of ancient stone.

This beautiful garden patio lies behind the 150-year-old Heritage House and next to the Robert Frost cottage. It was once the scene of congenial gatherings, including Frost, Tennessee Williams, Gloria Swanson and others.

The Autograph Tree

I don't keep a guest book for friends and visitors to my Southard Street home. Instead, I simply suggest they sign the autograph tree. Outside my gate, next to the street, is a pleasant tree whose low branches are an open invitation to small neighborhood tree climbers. Even more interesting are the leathery green 6-inch leaves just above the heads of pedestrians. Inscribed in tan lettering are quick thank you notes or goodbye's, some placed there nearly five years ago..

The autograph tree is scientifically known as *clusia rosea* and also goes by the name of pitch apple tree. It's considered an exotic, but common to the Caribbean region. With drought tolerance, salt resistance and preference for lower altitudes, it's a great shade tree for coastal areas.

Where the autograph custom arose I'm not sure, but it fits nicely into the friendly Key West ambiance. I tell my guests to simply write firmly with a ball point pen and, after a few days, inked lines are replaced with a scarred-over tan replica of the original message. An autograph tree will make an interesting addition to the front yard of your new Conch home, but be careful what you write. It will be there permanently.

The Mamey Tree

Fruit of Mamey tree (right).

As one would expect in America's only tropical corner, the visitor to Key West is treated to many new and unusual plant varieties. One is the Mamey tree. The handsome example pictured to the left stands near the old fire station on Virginia Street and was an early emigrant from Cuba. It is the largest in the United States and has long been a source of seedlings in efforts to introduce its species further north. *Mammea americana* is native to the West Indies and South America, but has had limited success in Central America, Africa and isolated parts of North America.

The fruit, brown and slightly oblong, ranges from 4 to 8 inches in diameter. Its ripe interior is fragrant and tastes somewhat like an apricot or raspberry.

Key Westers have always been fond of their Mamey tree and she rewards them each August with delicious fruit for ice cream desserts or salads. Like an old Cuban "abuela," she has nourished, entertained and been revered by many generations of Conchs.

Mango: *The Perfect Tree for a Conch Home's Back Yard*

Key West was the port through which tropical fruit was introduced to America. Ships' captains liked to outdo each other in acquiring the most exotic plants for their back yards. In an age before supermarket items we take for granted today, these were desirable plants for nourishment, vitamins, cleaning, and even medicines. For the mango, it was primarily the sheer delicious taste. Nothing makes you feel you've arrived in the tropics more than the taste of a ripe, delicious mango for breakfast---or anytime the mood hits.

You can judge a ripe mango by color and feel. The fruit, larger than an orange and smaller than a grapefruit, is primarily green, acquiring a strong reddish blush when ripe. To enjoy the mango year 'round, some residents like to can them, using the mango chutney recipe below.

Rosa's Mango Chutney

2 semi-ripe sweet mangoes
2 cups brown sugar
2-1/2 cups apple cider vinegar
1/4 cup key lime juice
2 tbsp finely chopped ginger

6 garlic cloves finely chopped
1 cup raisins
1 tsp hot chili flakes
1 tsp cumin
1/2 tsp sea salt
1/4 tsp ground cinnamon

Peel and chop mangoes, place in a bowl, sprinkle with salt, and let sit for one hour. Drain. Sprinkle mangoes with lime juice. Mix sugar and vinegar in a sauce pan and bring to a boil. Stir occasionally until sugar has dissolved. Carefully add mangoes, remaining ingredients and spices. Stir frequently until chutney is thick and dark. Chutney will keep for up to two weeks covered in the fridge. Makes three cups.

PLANT HARDINESS ZONES
(US Department of Agriculture)

The chart below shows zones for plants described on the following pages.

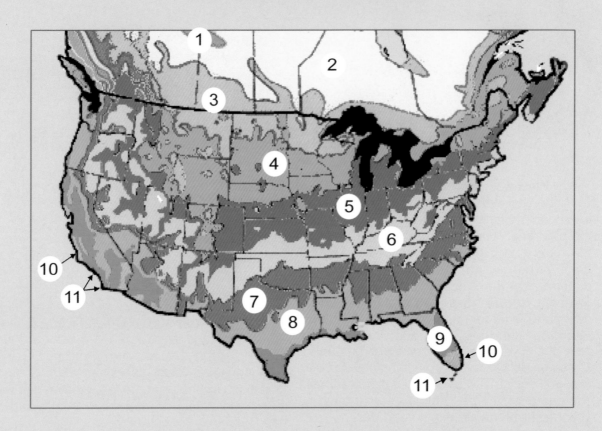

Average Annual
Minimum Temperature

Zone	Temperature
1	Below -50 F
2	-50 F to -40 F
3	-40 F to -30 F
4	-30 F to -20 F
5	-20 F to -10 F
6	-10 F to 0 F
7	0 F to 10 F
8	10 F to 20 F
9	20 F to 30 F
10	30 F to 40 F

FLOWERING TREES

**Kapok Tree
Floss SilkTree
(13)**

**Orchid Tree
Hong Kong Orchid
   Mountain Ebony
Ox's Hook
(15)**

**Bottle-Brush Tree
Weeping Bottle Brush
(4)**

**Yellow Elder
(20)**

**Royal Poinciana
Flame Tree
(17)**

**Frangipani
Pagoda Tree
(8)**

**Jacaranda
(11)**

		Zone
1. Acacia	*Acasia auriculaeformis*	10
2. African Tulip Tree, Flame of the Forest	*Spathodea campanulata*	10-11
3. Autograph Tree, Pitch Apple	*Clusia rosea*	10-11
4. Bottle-Brush Tree, Weeping Bottle Brush	*Callistemon rigidus*	9-11
5. Buttercup Tree	*Cochiospermum vitifolium*	10-11
6. Cajeput	*Melaleuca leucadendra*	9-11
7. Crabclaw Coral Tree	*Erythima indica*	10-11
8. Frangipani, Pagoda Tree	*Plumeria rubra*	10
9. Geiger Tree, Geranium Tree	*Cordia sebestena*	10-11
10. Golden Shower, Pudding Pipe Tree	*Cassia fistula*	9-10
11. Jacaranda	*Jacaranda mimosaefolla*	9-11
12. Jerusalem Thorn	*Parkinsonia aculeata*	8-11
13. Kapok Tree, Floss Silk Tree	*Chorisia speciosa*	9-11
14. Mahoe, Cuban Blast	*Hibiscus elatus*	10-11
15. Orchid Tree, Hong Kong Orchid Mountain Ebony, Ox's Hoof	*Bauhinia variegata, var. Candida*	9-10
16. Red Silk Cotton, Bombax	*Bombax malabaricum,*	
17. Royal Poinciana, Flame Tree	*Delonix regia*	10-11
18. Sausage Tree	*Kigelia pinnata*	10-11
19. Shaving Brush Tree	*Bombax ellipticum*	10-11
20. Yellow Elder	*Tecoma stans*	10-11

PALM TREES

Foxtail (10)

Coconut (7)

Royal (15)

Christmas (6)

Washington (17)

Travelers Tree (20)

Bismarck Palm (2)

Canary Island Date (4)

Cuban Pitticoat (8)

Alexander (1)

		Zone
1. Alexander Palm	*Ptychosperma elegans*	10-11
2. Bismarck Palm	*Bismarckia nobilis*	10-11
3. Cabbage Palm	*Sabal palmetto*	8-11
4. Canary Island Date Palm	*Phoenix canariensis*	9-10
5. Carpentaria	*Carpentaria acuminata*	10
6. Christmas Palm	*Veitchia merrill adonidia*	10-11
7. Coconut Palm	*Cocos nucifera*	10
8. Cuban Pitticoat Palm	*Copernicia macroglossa*	10-11
9. Fishtail Palm	*Caryota mitis*	9-10
10. Foxtail Palm	*Wodyetia bifurcata*	10-11
11. Florida Thatch Palm	*Thrinax floridana*	10-11
12. Florida Silver Palm	*Coccothrinax argentata*	10-11
13. Madagascar Palm, Areca	*Chrysalidocarpus lutescens*	10-11
14. Queen Palm	*Arecastrum*	9-10
15. Royal Palm	*Roystonea elata*	10
16. Sabal Palm	*Sabal palmetto*	8-10
17. Washington Palm	*Washintonia robusta*	8-10

Palm-Like Trees

18. Sago	*Cycas revoluta*	9-10
19. Screw Pine	*Pandanus utilis*	10
20. Travelers Tree	*Ravenala madagascariensis*	10

FRUIT TREES

Mamey (8)

Papaya (10)

Citrus: orange, lemon grapefruit (5)

Banana (2)

Sapodilla (11)

Sea Grape (12)

Mango (9)

		Zones
1. Avocado	*Persea americana*	9-10
2. Banana	*Musaceae musa*	9-10
3. Barbados Cherry	*Malpighia glabra*	10-11
4. Calamondin	*Citrus mitis*	9-10
5. Citrus; orange lemon, grapefruit	*Citrus rutaceae*	9-11
6. Key Lime	*Citrus aurantifolia*	10
7. Kumquat	*Fortunella margarita*	8-10
8. Mamey	*Mammea americana*	10-11
9. Mango	*Mangifera indica*	10-11
10. Papaya	*Carica papaya*	10-11
11. Sapodilla	*Manilkara zapota*	10-11
12. Sea Grape	*Coccolobis uvifera*	10-11
13. Surinam Cherry	*Eugenia uniflora*	10-11
14. Tamarind	*Tamarindus indica*	10-11

TREES: General

Norfolk Pine (14)

Banyon (3)

Spanish Lime (17)

Australian Pine (2)

Buttonwood (5)

Geiger (8)

Mahogany (12)

1.	Aralia	*Polyscias*	10-11
2.	Australian Pine	*Casuarina equisetifolia*	9-11
3.	Banyon	*Ficus benghalensis*	10-11
4.	Black Olive	*Bucida buceros*	10-11
5.	Buttonwood	*Conocarpus erustus*	10-11
6.	Florida Cork, Seside Mahoe	*Thespesia populnea*	10-11
7.	Florida Live Oak	*Quercus virginiana*	(all)
8.	Geiger	*Cordia sebestena*	10-11
9.	Gumbo Limbo	*Bursera simaruba*	10-11
10.	Jamaica Dogwood	*Piscidia piscipula*	11
11.	Lignum Vitae	*Guaiacum sanctum*	10-11
12.	Mahogany	*Swietenia mahogani*	10-11
13.	Mastic	*Mastichodendron foetidissimum*	10-11
14.	Norfolk Pine	*Araucaria heterophylla*	9-11
15.	Pigeon Plum	*Cocoloba diversifolia*	9-11
16.	Slash Pine, Dade Co. Pine	*Pinus elliottii*	8-10
17.	Spanish Lime	*Mamoncilla*	10-11
18.	Weeping Fig	*Ficus benjamina*	10-11

TALL SHRUBS

Bird of Paradise (2)

Lady of the Night (19)

Cocoplum (10)

Croton (12)

		Zone
1. Angel's Trumpet	*Datura arborea*	5-10
2. Bird of Paradise	*Strelitzea*	9-11
3. Barbados Flower-Fence Dwarf Poinciana	*Poinciana pulcherrima*	8-11
4. Bleeding Heart, Glory Bower	*Clerodendrum thomsoniae*	10-11
5. Calliandra, Powder Puff	*Calliandra surinamensis*	10-11
6. Candle Bush	*Cassia alata*	10-11
7. Cape Honeysuckle	*Tecomaria capensis*	9-11
8. Cardinal's Guard, Firespike	*Adontonema strictum*	8-11
9. Chinese Hat Plant, Parasol Plant	*Holmskioldia sanguinea*	10-11
10. Cocoplum	*Chrysobalanus icaco*	9-11
11. Crape Myrtle	*Lagerstroemia indica*	8-10
12. Croton	*Codiaeum variegatum*	9-10
13. Dracena	*Dracaena fragrans*	10-11
14. Gardenia	*Gardenia jasminoides*	8-10
15. Golden Dewdrop, Pigeon-berry	*Duranta repens*	9-11
16. Heliconia	*Heliconia bihai*	10-11
17. Hibiscus	*Hibiscus rosa-sinensis*	9-10
18. Jungle Flame Ixora	*Ixora coccinea*	10-11
19. Lady of the Night	*Brunsfelsia americana*	10
20. Oleander, Rose Bay	*Nerium oleander*	8-10
21. Orange Jasmine	*Murraya paniculata*	9-11
22. Plumbago	*Plumbago capensis*	8-11
23. Poinsettia	*Euphorbia pulcherrima*	9-11
24. Red Plume Ginger	*Alpinia purpurata*	10-11
25. Rubber Vine	*Cryptostegia madagascarensis*	10-11
26. Shell Ginger	*Apinia speciosa, alpinia zerumbet*	9-11
27. Spanish Bayonet	*Yucca aloifolia*	8-11
28. White Ixora	*Ixora finlaysoniana*	10-11

Photos courtesy of Master Gardener Landscaping of Fort Lauderdale; www.mgonline.com

Poinsettia (23)

Gardenia (14)

Hibiscus (17)

Jungle Flame Ixora (18)

SMALL SHRUBS

Aloe (1)

Crown of Thorns (6)

Coral Plant,
Firecracker Plant (4)

		Zone
1. Aloe	*Aloe barbadensis*	10-11
2. Billbergia	*Billbergia pyramidalis*	10
3. Carrion Flower	*Stapelia gigantea pallida*	9-11
4. Coral Plant, Firecracker Plant	*Russelia equisetiformis*	9-11
5. Crinum Lily, Milk-and-Wine Lily	*Crinum asiaticum*	9-11
6. Crown of Thorns	*Euporbia milii*	10-11
7. Dwarf Pomegranate	*Punica granatum*	8-11
8. Fairy Lily, Zephyr Flower, Rain Lily	*Zephyranthes*	8-11
9. Life Plant	*Kalanchoe gastonis-bonnieri*	10-11
10. Oyster Plant, Moses in the Bullrushes	*Rhoeo discolor*	9-10
11. Pentas, Starcluster	*Pentas lanceolata*	8-11
12. Periwinkle	*Catharanthus roseus*	9-11
13. Shrimp Plant	*Justicia brandegeana*	9-10
14. Spathiphyllum Patinii	*Spathiphyllum patinii*	10
15. Thryallis	*Galphima glauca*	9-11
16. Trailing Lantana, Weeping Lantana	*Lantana montevidensis*	8-11
17. Walking Iris, Fan Iris	*Neomarica longifolia*	10-11

Photos courtesy of Master Gardener Landscaping of Fort Lauderdale; www.mgonline.com

Periwinkle (12)

Shrimp Plant (13)

Thryallis (15)

DECORATIVE VINES

Bougainvillia (3)

Pandorea (9)

Alamanda (1)

Bleeding Heart
Glory Bower (2)

		Zone
1. Alamanda	*Allamanda cathartica*	9-10
2. Bleeding Heart Glorybower	*Clerodendrum thomsoniae*	10
3. Bougainvillea	*Bougainvillea glabra*	9-10
4. Chalice Vine, Cup of Gold	*Solandra guttata*	10-11
5. Confederate Jasmine	*Trachelospermum jasminoides*	8-10
6. Coralita, Coral Vine	*Antigonon leptopus*	9-10
7. Philodendron	*Philodendron hastatum*	10-11
8. Groundsel, Orange Glowvine, Mexican Flame Vine	*Senecio confusus*	10-11
9. Pandorea	*Podranea jasminoides*	10-11
10. Passion Flower Vine	*Passiflora*	9-11
11. Poet's Jasmine, Star Jasmine	*Jasinum grandiflorum*	9-11
12. Queen's Wreath, Sandpaper Vine	*Petrea volubilis*	10-11
13. Rangoon Creeper	*Quisqualis indica*	10-11
14. Stephanotis, Madagascar Jasmine	*Stephanotis floribunda*	10-11

Photos courtesy of Master Gardener Landscaping of Fort Lauderdale; www.mgonline.com

Philodendron (7)

Queen's Wreath,
Sandpaper Vine
(12)

Chalice Vine,
Cup of Gold
(4)

Stephanotis,
Madagascar
Jasmine (14)

Chapter 18

Checklist for
New Home Builders

You may already know that building a new home can be a stressful event. On average it costs 10 to 15% more than anticipated, but many headaches are eliminated by devoting a lot of attention to the planning stage. Here is a checklist to help get you started.

What are your present and future needs?

You may have seen a house on these pages that caught your fancy, but before getting locked in, step back and examine your lifestyle and needs. Is this a starter home or one you will occupy for decades? Are you a minimalist at heart or one who enjoys a large, rambling property? Is the size of your family expanding or shrinking? You don't want to become a maintenance slave, but don't overlook future requirements either. Remember, most people err on the side of too small.

What style is right for you?

The Conch homes in this book exude a unique warmth and tradition, but there is a considerable variety of styles. Does the Tennessee Williams cottage inspire you, do you yearn for a rambling mansion or want something a bit more contemporary? It may seem obvious, but this is an important question to answer before proceeding to interior layouts.

Interior Rooms and Layout

Early and thoughtful consideration allows your interior design to come together smoothly.

Decide on the number of stories:
single	
multiple	

Establish the exterior architectural style.
This could influence your interior choices:
cottage	
traditional	
contemporary	
victorian	
other	

Gathering Space Rooms:

formal parlor	_____
separate living room/family room	_____
one common great room	_____
fireplace/wood burning stove	_____
entertainment center/prewires	_____
built-in cabinets/glass display	_____
shelves/lighted shelves	_____
furniture arrangement; couch/	_____
loveseat/sectionals	
wet bar	_____
adjacent to outdoor space	_____
location to take advantage of views	_____
vaulted ceilings/tray ceilings	_____

Kitchen:

work triangle configuration/	_____
traffic flow	
walk-in pantry/utility closet	_____
sinks: single/double/drainboard/	_____
separate utility sink/	_____
stainless or porcelain	_____
appliance configuration:	
refrigerator; side-by-side,	_____
separate, freezer up/down,	_____
door dispensers	
freezer	_____
dishwasher; standard, drawer style	_____
range	_____
cooktop; no. of burners, grill	_____
ovens; wall, single or double	_____
microwave/advantium oven	_____
disposal	_____
trash compactor	_____
wine cooler	_____
ice maker	_____
water filter system	_____
instant/in-line water heater	_____
venting hoods	_____
warming ovens	_____
small appliances in garage/	_____
work center	
work island	_____
eat-at-bar; counter height/bar	_____
height/table height	
peninsula/island	_____
natural lighting; window/skylight	_____
ceiling height	_____
adjacent breakfast nook	_____
special considerations for	_____
frequent dinner parties	
desk/computer area	_____
mail/phone area	_____
cookbook shelf space	_____

Dining Room:

      formal/separate room   [   ]

      informal/open space   [   ]

      seating capacity/table size   [   ]

      furniture/cabinet consideration [   ]

Bedrooms:

Master Bedroom

      bed/furniture space allocation [   ]

      TV/media area [   ]

      wet bar/breakfast bar [   ]

      fireplace [   ]

      sitting area [   ]

      closets: walk-in/separate/wall [   ]

      built-in storage [   ]

      office/desk area [   ]

      reading lighting [   ]

      location relative to other rooms/ [   ]

      sound barriers/privacy [   ]

Other Bedrooms

      number/size/bed configurations [   ]

      location for security/privacy [   ]
         of children

      location for noise consideration/ [   ]
         floor levels

Bathrooms:

Master Bath

      1 or 2 vanities [   ]

      vanity/make-up table [   ]

      separate toilet/bidet area [   ]

      spa tub [   ]

      shower/steam shower [   ]

      shower: glass wall/tile wall [   ]

      natural lighting; windows/ [   ]
         skylight

      ventilation/fans [   ]

      heaters; floor/wall/ceiling [   ]

      mirrors/magnifying mirrors [   ]

      towel racks [   ]

      linen/bath supplies closet [   ]

      medicine cabinets [   ]

Other Baths

      powder room/location for privacy [   ]

      adjacent to other bedrooms [   ]

      sharing between bedrooms [   ]

      provisions for overnight guests [   ]

Laundry Room/Mud Room/Utility Room:

washer/dryer configuration;
  stacked, normal, raised
laundry chute/laundry sorting area
folding area
ironing area
sewing area
closets
large utility sink
pet areas
bulk storage/freezer space
garbage/recycling area
"wet space" for feet/shoes/clothes
pet door

Other Rooms:

office
den
home theater
billiards room
study
library
hobby/craft/sewing room
game room
workshop
music room
meditation room
exercise room

Outdoor Spaces:

screen room
covered porches
open air patios
outdoor kitchen/grill space
outdoor seating/lounging
outdoor dining
swimming pool
hot tub/spa
access to bathroom/shower
TV/media access

Detailed Decisions:

Exterior Walls

wood frame or concrete block
ceiling heights
siding (wood, artificial wood,
  lapped, novelty,
  board and batten, brick,
  stucco, rock)

External Doors

single or double
sidelights
transom

French (No. of panes)   [_____]
sliding/pocket   [_____]
wood, fiberglass, metal   [_____]

Countertops:
laminate   [_____]
tile   [_____]
marble (real or manufactured) [_____]
granite   [_____]
edge options   [_____]
tile backsplash   [_____]

Cabinets:
wood or laminate   [_____]
knobs or drawer pulls   [_____]
glass doors   [_____]
roll out shelves   [_____]
European (concealed hinges)   [_____]
recycle bins   [_____]

Walls:
drywall   [_____]
traditional 4 in. board or tongue   [_____]
   and groove
wallpaper, wallpaper borders [_____]

Floors:
solid wood: pine, oak, parquet, other
   wood laminates   [_____]
tile; laminates, slate, ceramic, brick [_____]
vinyl   [_____]
carpeting: plush, berber, sculptured,   [_____]
   wool, nylon, acrylic

Windows:
single or double hung   [_____]
casement   [_____]
wood, vinyl clad   [_____]
single, double, triple glass [_____]
number of panes   [_____]
skylights   [_____]
bay   [_____]

Shutters:
side hinged: louver, vertical boards [_____]
Bahama top hinged   [_____]
doors and windows   [_____]

Ceilings:
drywall   [_____]
wood: tongue and groove, plank [_____]
coffered/tray   [_____]
flat   [_____]
exposed beam/rafters   [_____]

ceiling fans   ☐

antique stamped panels   ☐

Interior Trim:

paint or stain   ☐

cased entry ways   ☐

cased windows   ☐

crown mold   ☐

chair rail   ☐

picture panel   ☐

plate rail   ☐

built ins   ☐

door style   ☐

Bathroom Details:

tub, shower, spa   ☐

toilet, bidet   ☐

sinks, faucets   ☐

built ins, closets   ☐

Lighting:

fixtures   ☐

indirect   ☐

track   ☐

display   ☐

landscape   ☐

Roof:

metal (V-crimp, or tile)   ☐

asphalt shingle   ☐

gabled venting or ridge venting   ☐

Mechanical Systems:

heat source (gas, forced air, heat
pump, hot water, radiant heat)   ☐

air conditioning   ☐

whole house fan   ☐

air cleaner   ☐

humidifier   ☐

water heater   ☐

recirculating pump   ☐

electrical, phone, cable   ☐

intercom and security system   ☐

wall vacuum   ☐

Chapter 19

Obtaining Products and Services

Planning your new home or renovation is likely to
take your search beyond the local lumber yard and hardware store. To aid in your quest, here is a list of resources. Along with contact information for major manu-
facturers of building components, there are sources for
many unique and hard to locate items. These include
specialty products such as authentic Key West gingerbread, extremely low maintenance decking and siding,
and reclaimed or distressed wood.

Antique Hardware
House of Antique Hardware   www.HouseofAntiqueHardware.com

Cabinetry
Crownpoint Cabinetry   1-800-999-4994
                            www.crown-point.com

Wellborn Cabinet, Inc.   1-800-336-8040
                            www.wellborn.com

Wood-Mode Cabinetry   www.wood-mode.com

Rutt Handcrafted Cabinetry 1-800-220-7888
                            www.rutt.net

Fieldstone Cabinetry, Inc. 1-800-339-5369
                            www.FieldstoneCabinetry.com

Ceilings
Tin Ceilings: Aa-abbingdon 1-718-258-8333
        Affiliates, Inc.   www.abbingdon.com

Chelsea Decorative Metal   1-713-721-9200
                            www.thetinman.com

M-Boss Inc.   1-866-886-2677
                            www.mbossinc.com

Doors

Pinecrest	1-612-871-7071	
	www.pinecrestinc.com	
I.W.P. Doors	1-800-468-3667	
	www.iwpdoor.com	
Hendricks Woodworking	1-610-756-6187	
	www.historicdoors.com	
Therma-Tru Doors	1-800-843-7628	
	www.thermatru.com	
Coppa Woodworking, Inc.	1-310-548-5332	
	www.coppawoodworking.com	
Designer Doors	1-800-910-9976	
	www.designerdoors.com	

Exterior Decking/Railing

CertainTeed "Evernew"	1-800-233-8990	Composite and vinyl decking,
	www.certainteed.com	fencing, railing and siding
Woodway Products	1-800-459-8718	Lattice, deckrails, post
	www.woodwayproducts.com	caps, planking
Trex Company	1-800-289-8739	Wood and composite
	www.trex.com	decking and railing
Tendura	1-800-836-3872	Decking, composite
	www.tendura.com	plastic, vinyl

Gutters

Classic Gutter Systems	1-269-382-2700
	www.classicgutters.com

Key West Gingerbread

Hansen & Bringle Cabinet and Millwork	1-305-294-4279	Custom and standard Key
	hbcabinet@bellsouth.com	Key West patterns
The Plastic Trading Company	1-561-840-9494	Standard Key West patterns
	www.plastictrading.com	in plastic

Lighting

Rejuvenation	1-888-401-1900
	www.rejuvenation.com
Metropolitan Artifacts	1-770-986-0007
	www.metropolitanartifacts.com
Luminaria Lighting, Inc.	1-800-638-5619
	www.luminaria.com
Lighting by Hammerworks	1-508-755-3434
	www.hammerworks.com
Victorian Lighting Works	1-814-364-9577
	www.vlworks.com

Mantels

Mantels of Yesteryear   1-706-492-5534
                        www.mantelsofyesteryear.com

Outdoor Lawn Fixtures & Furniture

Country Casual   1-800-284-8325
                        www.countrycasual.com

Walpole Woodworkers   1-800-343-6948

Patio/Paver Stones:

Belgard   1-877-235-4273
                        www.belgardhardscapes.com

Plumbing

Renovators   1-800-659-0203
                        www.rensup.com

Vintage Tub & Bath   1-877-868-1369
                        www.vintagetub.com

St. Thomas Creations   1-619-336-3980
                        www.stthomascreations.com

Kohler   1-800-456-4537
                        www.kohler.com

Reclaimed Lumber/Wood Flooring-Heart Pine, Dade Co. Pine and More

Albany Woodworks   1-800-551-1282
                        www.albanywoodworks.com

A. L. Roy Lumber Co., Inc.   www.roylumber.com

Antique Building Materials   www.antiquebuilding materials.com

Appalachian Woods   www.appalachianwoods.com
  Antique Flooring

Authentic Pine Floors   1-800-283-6038
                        www.authenticpinefloors.com

Cape Fear Heart Pine   www.capefearheartpine.com

E.T. Moore, Inc.   www.etmoore.com

Heartwood Associates   www.heartwoodassociates.com

Hill Country Woodworks   www.texaswoodwork.com
  of Texas

James and Co.   www.jamesandcompany.com

Longleaf Lumber   www.longleaflumber.com

Mountain Lumber Company 1-800-445-2671
                        www.mountainlumber.com

Lumber Liquidators   1- 877-645-5347
                        www.lumberliquidators.com

Pine Tree Builders	1-800-383-5598 www.pinetreebuilders.com	
Carlisle Restoration Lumber	1-800-595-9663 www.wideplankflooring.com	
Goodwin Heart Pine	1-800-336-3118 www.heartpine.com	
Bear Creek Lumber	1-800-597-7191 www.bearcreeklumber.com	
Resource Recovery	www.heartpine.org	
Sawmill Treasures	www.sawmilltreasures.com	
The Heart Pine Flooring Co.	www.riverbottompineflooring.com	
Vintage Lumber Sales	www.vintagelumbersales.com	
Whiskey Wood	www.whiskeywood.com	
Will Branch Antique Lumber	www.willbranch.net	

Renovation and New Construction Services

J.J. Fairbanks Construction Services	305-292-6584	Historic renovation specialist
Mark Thomas	305-304-5097	Spiral staircase specialist

Roofing

McElroy Metal, Inc.	1-800-950-6533 www.mcelroymetal.com	
Fabral	1-800-477-2741 www.fabral.com	
Wheeling Corrugating Co.	www.wheelingcorrugating.com	
Atas- Advanta Shingle	1-800-468-1441 www.atas.com	
Berridge Manufacturing Co.	1-800-231-8127 www.berridge.com	Copies of Key West metal shingles from the 1800s
Metal Construction Assoc.	www.metalconstruction.org	Information on metal roof styles and manufacturers
Southeastern Metals Manufacturing Co., Inc.	1-904-757-4200	V-crimp metal panels

Salvaged Components

Southern Accents	1-877-737-0554	

Siding

James Hardie Siding Products	1- 800-JHARDIE www.jameshardie.com	Low maintenance simulated wood siding

Specialty Trim

HB & G Columns	1-800-264-4424 www.hbgcolumns.com	
Outwater Architectural Products	1-800-835-4400 www.outwater.com	Moldings, ceiling medallions columns, etc.
Cinder Whit & Company	1-800-527-9064 www.cinderwhit.com	Porch posts, ballusters, finials, etc.
Chadsworth's Columns	1-800-486-2118 www.columns.com	Columns, decorative capitals
Worthington Architectural Details	1-800-872-1608 www.worthingtononline.com	
Melton Classics, Inc.	1-800-963-3060 www.meltonclassics.com	Columns, ballustrades
Decra Mold, Kay-Wood Industries, Inc.	1-800-654-4535 www.decramold.com	Molding, mantels

Vintage Appliances

Heartland Appliances, Inc.	1-800-361-1517 www.heartlandapp.com	

Windows

Andersen Windows & Doors	1-800-426-4261 www.andersenwindows.com	
Marvin Windows & Doors	1-800-268-7644 www.marvin.com	
Pella Corporation	1- 888-847-3552 www.pella.com	
Pozzi Wood Windows	1-800-257-9663 www.pozzi.com	
Kolbe & Kolbe Millwork Company, Inc.	1-715-842-5666 www.kolbe-kolbe.com	

Window Shutters

Timberlane Woodcrafters	1-800-250-2221 www.timberlanewoodcrafters.com	Stock and custom shutters
Pinecrest	1-612-871-7071 www.pinecrestinc.com	Doors, shutters, stamped ceiling and wall panels
Shuttercraft, Inc.	1-203-245-2608 www.shuttercraft.com	Interior, exterior shutters

Chapter 20

Choosing Your Building Plans

You've found the home of your dreams! The street-side facade and interior/exterior spaces are unique, yet it possesses classic qualities that appealed to an earlier generation of Key West artists and writers. Picture yourself lounging on the veranda, enjoying the ocean view and waving to admiring friends. Now it's time to turn the fantasy into reality!

If you're one of the millions of Americans considering new home construction, your first order of business is obtaining house plans. There are two options available: employ a professional building designer to produce a custom design or purchase a set of pre-designed building plans that meet your requirements. Cost is the obvious motivator for buying plans. Stock plans are available at 5% to 20% of the fee charged by professionals. An additional consideration is that stock plans represent a well-engineered design that has usually been proven by other satisfied customers. If a building design that appeals to you requires minor modification to achieve everything you desire, you're still far ahead of the game.

Whether it's a Classic Conch house or a more contemporary version, your plans can be quickly pro-

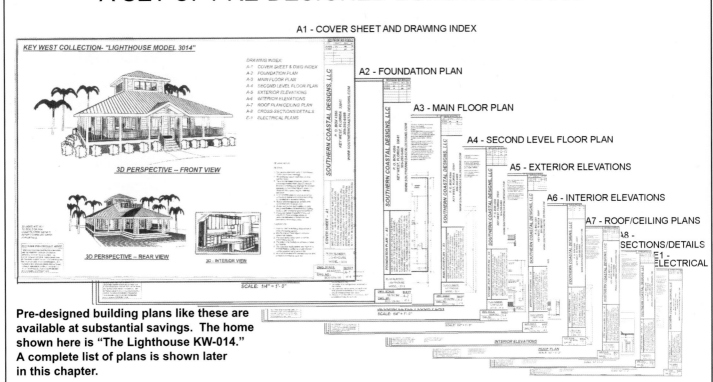

A SET OF PRE-DESIGNED BUILDING PLANS

Pre-designed building plans like these are available at substantial savings. The home shown here is "The Lighthouse KW-014." A complete list of plans is shown later in this chapter.

vided so you can begin the process. Armed with detailed documentation you're prepared to sit down with a builder to explore construction costs and schedules. The CAD (computer-aided design) package shown on the previous page rigorously documents every construction detail and contains drawings in a 1/4-inch to 1-foot scale.

The authors have distinguished careers as designers and engineers and employ the latest technology. The results are highly functional designs with creative approaches for modern urban living. All building plans described in this chapter meet nationally recognized codes and are engineered to withstand hurricane-force winds.

While developing a design they use 3D virtual modeling, which enables them to "walk through" homes complete with furniture, and wall and floor coverings. This assures that final plans are complete and accurate, and avoids unwanted surprises after the home is constructed. Such virtual modeling also produced the 3D exploded views in this book.

So, having found the coastal home of your dreams, and assured of a sound, well-engineered design, you're ready to make a selection.

Co-author Judi Sample Smith designs with software that provides realistic views of a home before it's constructed and a detailed package of plans for the builder. A member of the American Institute of Building Design, she is also co-founder of Southern Coastal Designs.

Key West House Plans

Classic Conch Houses	Identification No.
The Shotgun	KW-001
The One and One-Half	KW-002
The Cottage	KW-003
The Eyebrow	KW-004
The Temple	KW-005
The Conch Captain	KW-006
The Mansion	KW-007
The Queen Anne Victorian	KW-008
The Bahama	KW-009

Contemporary with a Key West Flair	
The Duval	KW-010
The Marquesa	KW-011
The Angela	KW-012
The Southard	KW-013
The Lighthouse	KW-014
The Olivia	KW-015

Ordering building plans is easy; contact:

Southern Coastal Designs, LLC
P.O. Box 4255
Key West, FL 33041
Tel: 1-800-355-8562

Visit our web site for additional selections:
www.southerncoastaldesigns.com

Appendix

Historic Key West
Gingerbread Patterns

The following pages illustrate all of the classic
"gingerbread" found around the historic district.
They include Ballusters, Brackets and Cornice trim.
All patterns are scaled on a 1-inch grid.

Ballusters

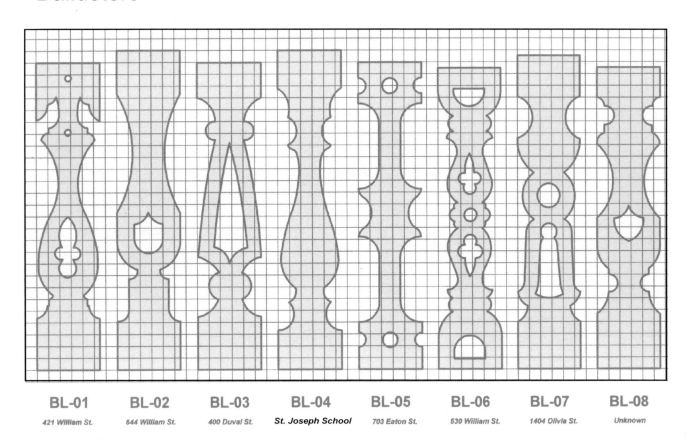

BL-01	BL-02	BL-03	BL-04	BL-05	BL-06	BL-07	BL-08
421 William St.	644 William St.	400 Duval St.	St. Joseph School	703 Eaton St.	530 William St.	1404 Olivia St.	Unknown

Ballusters

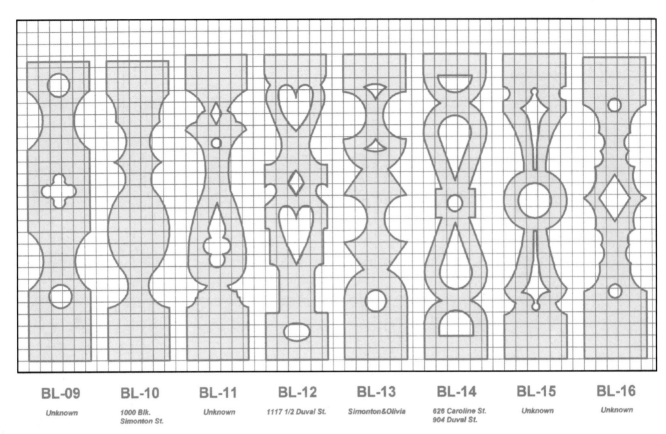

BL-09	BL-10	BL-11	BL-12	BL-13	BL-14	BL-15	BL-16
Unknown	*1000 Blk.* *Simonton St.*	*Unknown*	*1117 1/2 Duval St.*	*Simonton&Olivia*	*626 Caroline St.* *904 Duval St.*	*Unknown*	*Unknown*

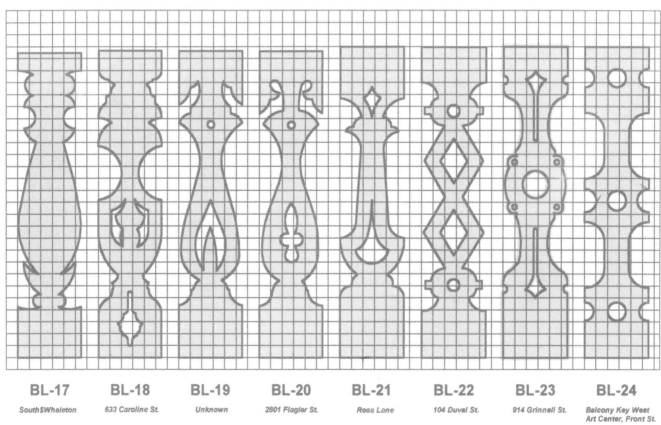

BL-17	BL-18	BL-19	BL-20	BL-21	BL-22	BL-23	BL-24
South$Whaleton	*633 Caroline St.*	*Unknown*	*2801 Flagler St.*	*Ross Lane*	*104 Duval St.*	*914 Grinnell St.*	*Balcony Key West* *Art Center, Front St.*

Ballusters

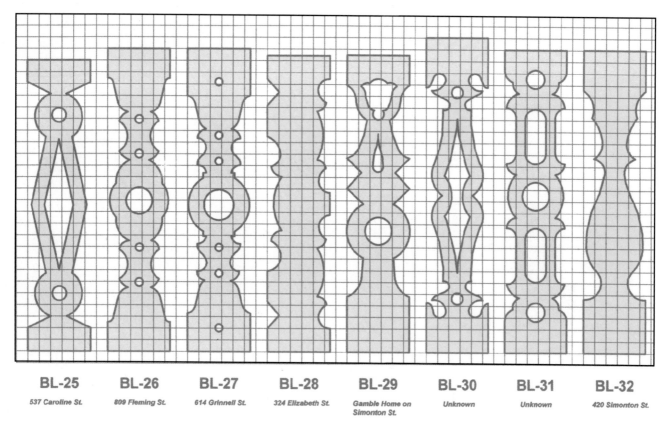

BL-25
537 Caroline St.

BL-26
809 Fleming St.

BL-27
614 Grinnell St.

BL-28
324 Elizabeth St.

BL-29
Gamble Home on Simonton St.

BL-30
Unknown

BL-31
Unknown

BL-32
420 Simonton St.

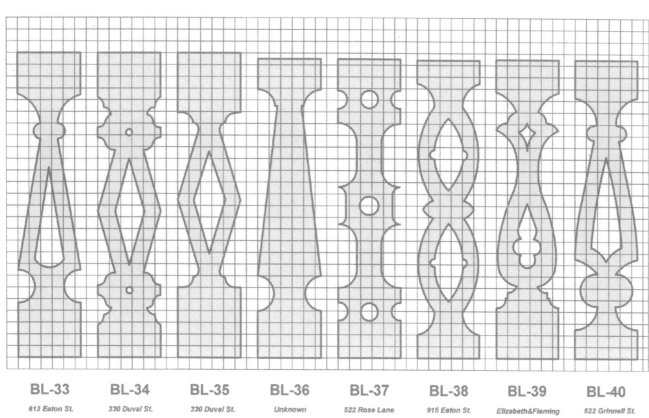

BL-33
613 Eaton St.

BL-34
330 Duval St.

BL-35
330 Duval St.

BL-36
Unknown

BL-37
522 Rose Lane

BL-38
915 Eaton St.

BL-39
Elizabeth&Fleming

BL-40
522 Grinnell St.

Ballusters

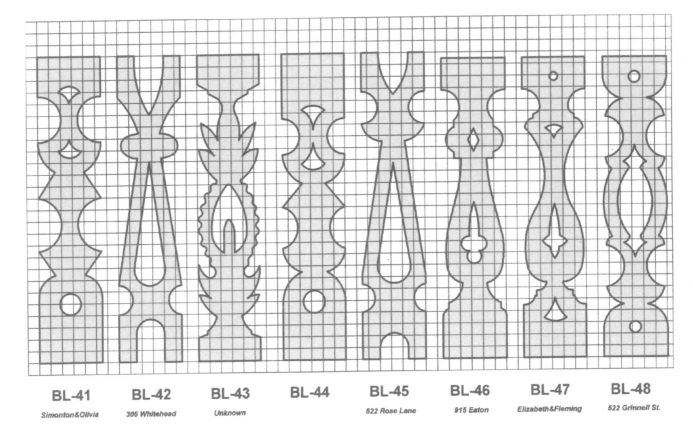

BL-41
Simonton&Olivia

BL-42
305 Whitehead

BL-43
Unknown

BL-44

BL-45
522 Rose Lane

BL-46
915 Eaton

BL-47
Elizabeth&Fleming

BL-48
522 Grinnell St.

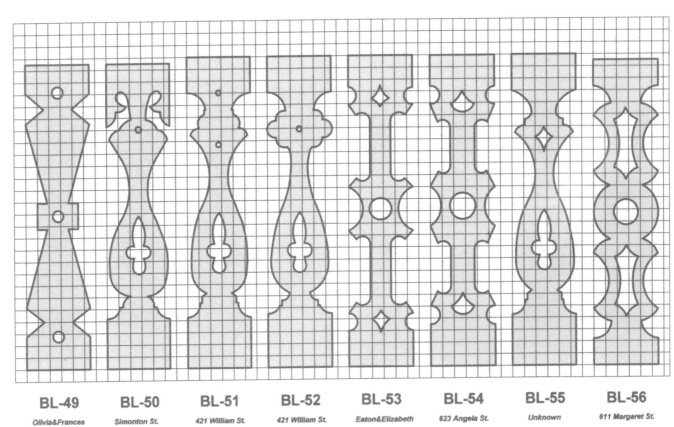

BL-49
Olivia&Frances

BL-50
Simonton St.

BL-51
421 William St.

BL-52
421 William St.

BL-53
Eaton&Elizabeth

BL-54
623 Angela St.

BL-55
Unknown

BL-56
611 Margaret St.

Ballusters

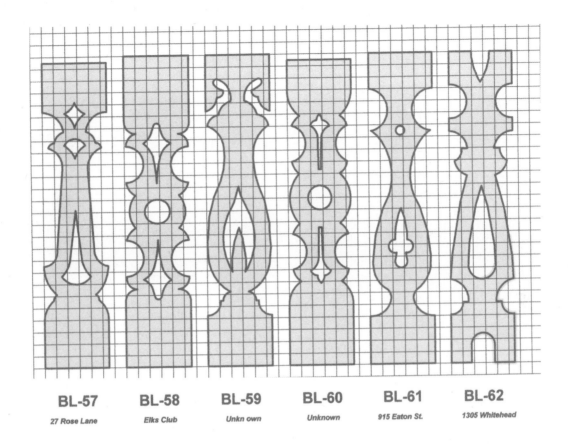

BL-57

27 Rose Lane

BL-58

Elks Club

BL-59

Unkn own

BL-60

Unknown

BL-61

915 Eaton St.

BL-62

1305 Whitehead

Brackets and Cornice Trim

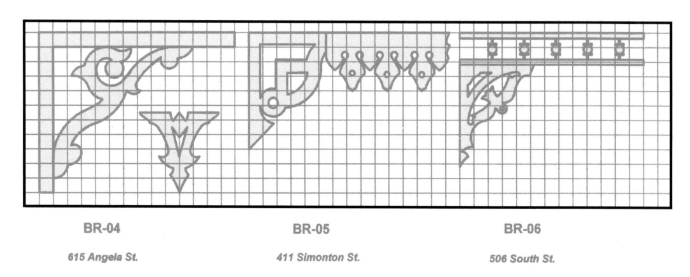

BR-04	BR-05	BR-06
615 Angela St.	411 Simonton St.	506 South St.

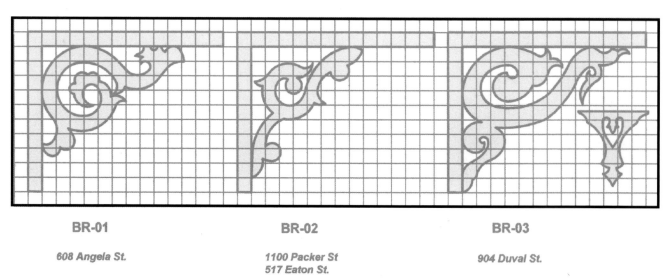

BR-01	BR-02	BR-03
608 Angela St.	1100 Packer St 517 Eaton St.	904 Duval St.

Scale: 1-inch grid

Brackets and Cornice Trim

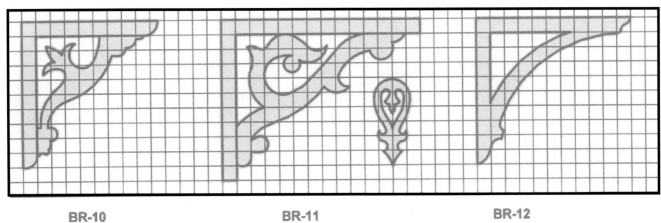

BR-10	**BR-11**	**BR-12**
716 Thomas St.	*504 Simonton St.* *504 Eaton St.* *517 Eaton St.*	*Elizabeth&Windsor Ln.*

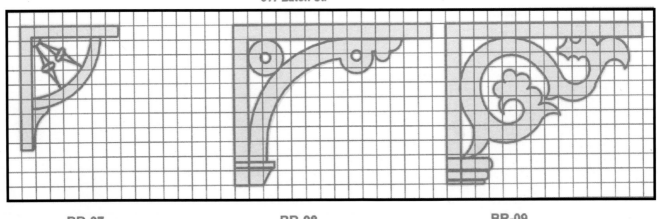

BR-07	**BR-08**	**BR-09**
Duval - Lopez Bldg.	*407 Whitehead St.*	*602 Southard St.*

Brackets and Cornice Trim

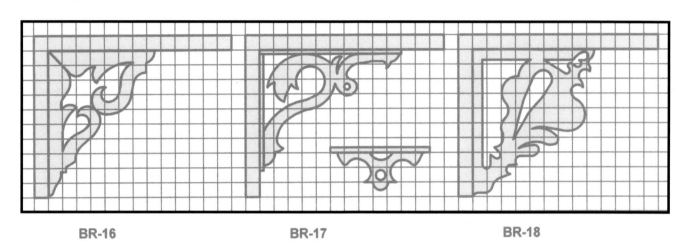

BR-16

700 Elizabeth St.

BR-17

1030 Fleming St.

BR-18

526 Southard St.

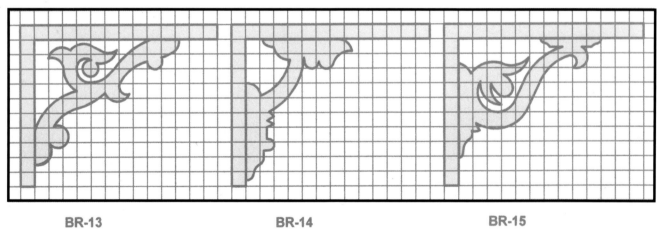

BR-13

1100 Duval St.

BR-14

919 Whitehead St.

BR-15

529 Simonton St.

Brackets and Cornice Trim

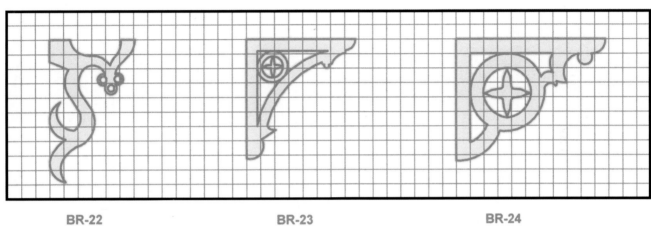

BR-22

507 Whitehead St.

BR-23

6 Truman St.

BR-24

707 Truman St.

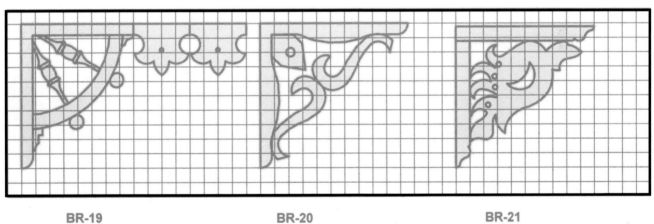

BR-19

320 Truman St.

BR-20

1525 Flagler St.

BR-21

1410 Duncan St.

Brackets and Cornice Trim

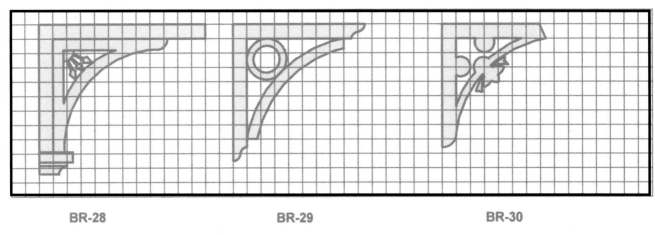

BR-28

426 Elizabeth St.

BR-29

6 Southard St.

BR-30

Eaton St. - Sawyer

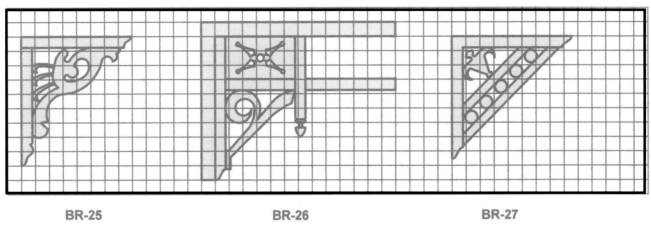

BR-25

1020 Southard St.

BR-26

529 Elizabeth St.

BR-27

401 Eaton St.

Brackets and Cornice Trim

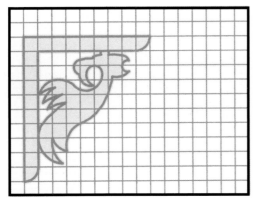

BR-32

925 Whitehead St.

BR-33

615 Elizabeth St.

BR-31

410 Simonton St.

Brackets and Cornice Trim

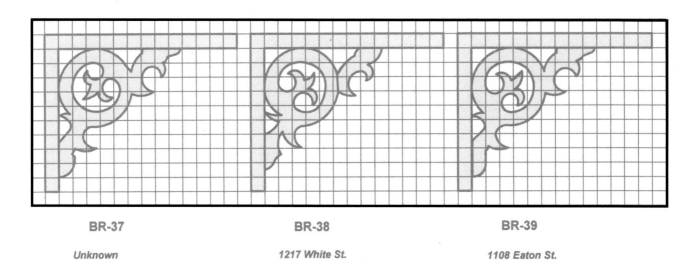

BR-37	BR-38	BR-39
Unknown	*1217 White St.*	*1108 Eaton St.*

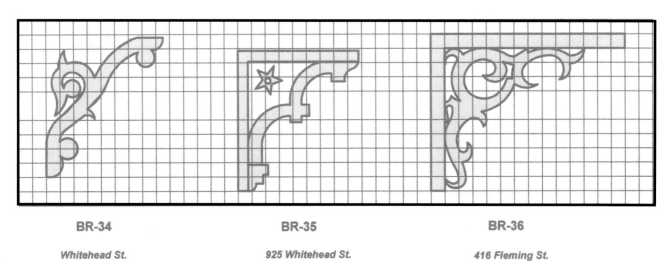

BR-34	BR-35	BR-36
Whitehead St. Cosgrove House	*925 Whitehead St.*	*416 Fleming St.*

Brackets and Cornice Trim

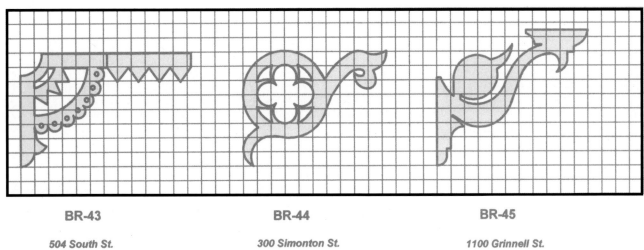

BR-43

504 South St.

BR-44

300 Simonton St.

BR-45

1100 Grinnell St.

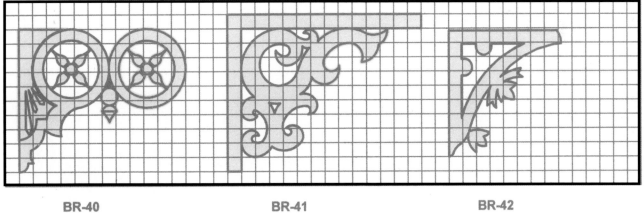

BR-40

814 Duval St.
915 Duval St.
1001 Eaton St.

BR-41

2801 Flagler St..

BR-42

1117 Varela St.

Brackets and Cornice Trim

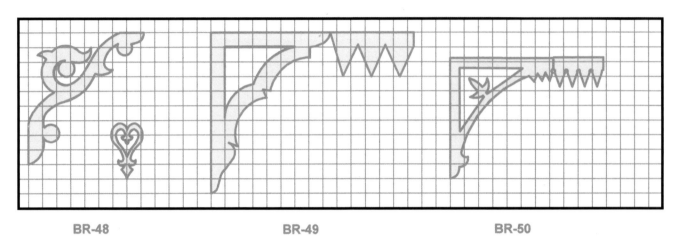

BR-48

1013 Truman St.

BR-49

506 Elizabeth St.

BR-50

323 Whitehead St.

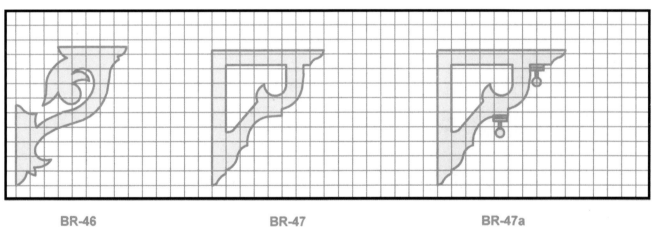

BR-46

1004 Packer St.

BR-47

61 Whitehead St.

BR-47a

*61 Whitehead St.
2nd Floor*

Brackets and Cornice Trim

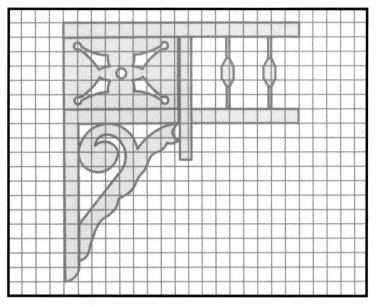

BR-57

Unknown

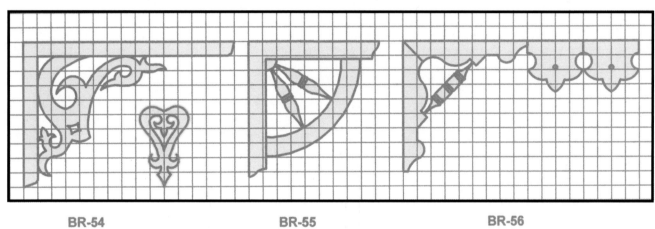

BR-54

705 Truman St.

BR-55

509 South St.

BR-56

320 Truman St.

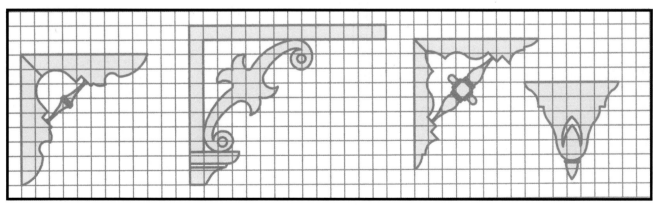

BR-51

508 Simonton St.
531 Simonton St.

BR-52

412 Elizabeth St..

BR-53

Unknown

Bibliography

Altobello, Patricia and Pierce, Deirdre. *Literary Sands of Key West*. Washington, D. C. 1996

Blumenson, John J.-G. *Identifying American Architecture*. New York. W.W. Norton & Company. 1977

Caemmerer, Alex. *The Houses of Key West*. Sarasota, Florida. Pineapple Press. 1992.

Carley, Rachel. *The Visual Dictionary of American Domestic Architecture*. New York.
    Henry Holt and Company. 1994

Cox, Christopher, *Key West Companion*, New York: St. Martin's Press, 1983

Frawley-Holler, Janis. *Gardens of Key West*. Sarasota, Florida. Pineapple Press. 2000

Haehle, Robert G. and Brookwell, Joan. *Native Florida Plants*. Houston. Gulf Publishing Company. 1999.

Harris, Cyril M. *American Architecture - An Illustrated Encyclopedia*. New York.
    W. W. Norton & Company. 1998

Historic Architectural Guidelines. City of Key West. 2002

The Key West Garden Club. *Where the Tropics Begin*. 1994

The Marathon Garden Club. *Fabulous Trees of the Fabulous Keys*. 1985.

McAlester, Virginia and Lee, *A Field Guide to American Houses*, New York: Alfred A. Knopf, 1990

Mitchell, James. *The Craft of Modular Post and Beam*. Vancouver. Hartley & Marks. 1984

Research Atlantica, Inc. *City of Key West, Florida Historic Site Survey*. 1998

Sobon, Jack and Schroeder, Roger. *Timber Frame Construction*. Vermont. Storey Books. 1984.

Starr, Roger, *The Carpenter-Architects of Key West* American Heritage Magazine, Volume 23,
    No. 2 (February, 1975)

Valle, Erick. *American Urban Typologies - Key West, Florida*. Miami. Village Publishers, Inc., 1995

Wells, Sharon and Lawson Little, *Portraits: Wooden Houses of Key West*. Key West, Florida:
    Historic Key West Preservation Board, 1982

Windhorn, Stan and Langley, Wright. *Yesterday's Key West*. Key West. Langley Press, Inc. 1999